Sometimes Things Fall Apart

Sometimes Things Fall Apart

A SPOUSE'S STORY ABOUT BLINDNESS, MENTAL ILLNESS, DISMANTLED BELIEFS, AND LIFE NOT GOING AS PLANNED

BECKY LEBLANC

Sometimes Things Fall Apart:
A Spouse's Story about Blindness, Mental Illness, Dismantled Beliefs, and Life Not Going as Planned

ISBN: 978-0-9759258-2-9 (softcover)
ISBN: 978-0-9759258-3-6 (eBook)
Library of Congress Control Number: 2025922436

Cover and Interior design: 1106 Design

Printed in the United States of America

For anyone whose life has ever fallen apart

AUTHOR'S NOTE

Before I began to write this book, I made a list of what I hoped readers might take away. My intentions for what you are about to read are listed below:

- I want to prove that hard stories can be beautifully written.
- I want spacious pages.
- I want to share knowledge about what a mental-health crisis looks like.
- I want those who can't talk about their own experiences yet to feel a rush of familiarity, to know that they are not alone, and that devastation can be survived.
- I want people to know they can change what they believe.
- I want to point out flawed beliefs and shallow comforts.
- I want people to know they can disappoint others and keep God.
- I want to humanize the experience of mental-health issues.
- I want to share parts of the experience through poetry.
- I want to create oxygen around the experience.

- Just when people feel about to cry, I want to make them laugh.
- I want to identify what's already beautiful.
- I want to tell the blindness story.
- I want to tell the mental-health story.
- I want to tell the faith story.
- I want to tell it in essays and poems.
- I want to weave the blindness, mental-health, and faith stories together.
- I want to shepherd people through it and leave them better.

TABLE OF CONTENTS

INTRODUCTION

This was not what I had planned for my life.

Don't get me wrong—I never had white-picket-fence dreams.

I went into our marriage fully aware that it would include physical disability. I knew while we were dating that he had a condition that would lead to blindness. Yet, as sad as the idea of impending blindness was, we both thought it would be inconvenient yet manageable.

What I did not anticipate were the mental-health issues in the form of psychosis and depression that would insert themselves into our lives fifteen years into our marriage. Mental-health issues made their arrival known, much like how I imagine an inebriated screech monkey carrying a bullhorn into a silent yoga retreat might present.

There was nothing subtle about it.

The mental-health issues were neither manageable nor convenient. When added to blindness, they were the catalyst that imploded our once-tidy lives and required a wholesale reset of everything we believed about how life works, how God works, how pretty much anything works.

But I'm getting ahead of myself.

Let's start with blindness.

Section I

Blindness

AT FIRST

It didn't matter to me that he was going blind. I was seventeen. He was twenty. He was funny, happy, and unbelievably kind—not just to me but to everyone around him. Right from the start, he was honest about being "legally blind" from a hereditary eye disease called Retinitis Pigmentosa (RP) that would take his remaining vision over the next few years. When he shared his diagnosis, I remember feeling a bit sad for him. But I don't remember feeling concerned for us.

I remember thinking, *This is the most positive, happy person that I've ever met.* He had already adapted to being legally blind at the age of twenty. He was working full-time at a bicycle shop. I was sure he would adapt just as well to whatever was coming in the future. We married eight years later. We took our time getting married because we were young and—as I like to say—I wanted to be sure there would be absolutely no surprises. This is so funny to me now.

I look back on my reaction to his blindness then and see how it was really focused on my total respect for him. I was in awe of how well he lived his life. If he needed something, he always found a way to get it. As an example, though he wasn't allowed to drive a car, he was adept at riding his mountain bike absolutely everywhere. During his wind-surfing stage, he even created a side trolley for his bike and rode himself, the bike, and the wind surfer right down to the beach whenever he wanted. I'd never met anyone who could problem-solve in quite the same way.

Plus, he was just plain fun. I am naturally a bit on the quiet side. My brother used to call me "The Thinker" because I spend a lot of time in my brain. So, Joe's lighthearted personality was like fresh air to me. Wherever he went, he brought the party, and I was happy to attend. With him, blindness seemed to be more of a background nuisance rather than anything that could hold him back. He never made blindness an issue, so it was easy to forget he had a vision problem at all. And if blindness wasn't going to be an issue for him, it certainly wasn't going to be one for me. Maybe it's like how you'd feel if you were going to meet a new friend for the first time and were taken aback at first to find out that he was in a wheelchair. It's a bit startling at first. Then, as you get to know the person and see him beautifully navigate life, what wells up within you is respect for the journey. After a while, you don't even notice the chair. After a while, I didn't notice the blindness.

I never once thought about how his diagnosis would impact me. Never once fast-forwarded to what our day-to-day life together might look like. I knew he didn't drive and that it could be an inconvenience. But I also saw how he compensated and found creative ways to get wherever he wanted to go. I wasn't worried about our future. He was a gem of a human, and I knew that, no matter what came our way, who he was would not change. I knew he would continue moving forward and get whatever he needed from life using his own ingenuity. I was sure of that.

At first, life didn't seem too hard. We found each other's company easy and fun. People used to think that was amazing. They would look at us as if we were doing something super-hard . . . being happy though one of us was going blind. It wasn't hard at all. We were simply happy.

But there was so much then that I just didn't know.

LATER ON

As the years went by, the losses became harder. It became clear that my respect for *his* ability to adapt wouldn't be enough to get us through. *I* also had to adapt. Daily.

As it turns out, disability in marriage is life-changing for both spouses. Oh, I know that people like to hear things such as, "Disability is no problem; we love each other, and that's all that matters." While that can be true at times, the reality is that *nothing* about being disabled or being married to someone with a disability is easy. It is hard. It is hard not seeing. It is also hard not to be seen. It is hard to see beauty and not be able to explain it well. It is hard to see a zillion-legged bug in the house and realize I might be in charge of dealing with it. It is hard to see parts of our house that need repair and figure out what's worth mentioning. It is hard that he can't read my facial expressions. It is hard to come home with a new hairstyle that only *I* can see. For the record, he always says, "Your hair looks amazing" when I come back from a haircut now, because he is funny, and he is no fool. It is hard to be the one who always gets up to get the extra napkins or utensils when we are out at breakfast. It is hard feeling responsible for our safety in crowds or simply remembering where our seats are at concerts. It is hard never getting to be the passenger. So, that "He Ain't Heavy" song lyric from the sixties was a flat-out lie. He is my husband, and he *is*, in fact, sometimes "*. . . heavy . . .*"

When you are young, newly married, and filled with youthful optimism, life's challenges are actually sweet. Neither of you has money, and it doesn't matter, because you have each other. You also have plenty of company, because other people your age—unless they've been given a hand up from their parents or a wealthy relative—also have nothing. There are no disparities among your group of friends. You are all equally broke and in the early stages of starting your careers. You have nothing except your happiness, and that's more than enough.

Maybe others could see into our future—see how hard things were going to get. Maybe they knew how, fifteen years later, loss would break us into pieces. Make the sweet life we once shared unrecognizable. I had no idea.

I underestimated how sad it would be to see things that Joe could not. No amount of descriptive words can make up for seeing. I used to rush to describe interesting things when we were out, but, now, I just silently take them in. The world is too big. There is too much to describe.

I also underestimated the hours I'd spend *waiting.* And I mean that literally. So much of my time was spent driving places to drop him off and pick him up. When he could, he took public transportation, but having me drive him places was always quicker, and, besides, what kind of wife says, "Hey, blind husband—head on down to the bus stop, and wait on the street in the rain, even though I'm at home, technically available to give you a ride"? I could lie and say it was no trouble, but, oftentimes, it *was* inconvenient for me. I spent a lot of time in my car, waiting for him to get out of work or finish up whatever he needed to finish. I learned to bring things to help me pass the time. This was well before smartphones, so I would bring books and sometimes wood-carving projects. The first ten years of this wasn't so bad. For anyone who likes a visual, please picture me saying this standing in three feet of wood shavings, with discarded books all around. Eventually, this routine got old. Time is precious. Who wants to spend hours a week waiting for someone else to do anything? I started to wonder, *What is it that I'd be doing right now if I weren't doing this? What hobby would I be pursuing? What thoughts would I be thinking? What dream would I be following if I weren't always stuck waiting?*

Things I Really Missed

Years into our marriage, I realized how different my life was. I missed the life I could have had. This doesn't mean I don't love Joe. It means I'm being honest about life with a disabled spouse.

Here is a partial list of the things I really missed:

- *The feeling—even for a minute—that "it's all going to be okay"*
  No one can tell me it's all going to be okay. It's going to be okay only if I make it so. We are going to stay above water financially only if I make it so, either by cutting an expense, arranging a payment plan, or bringing in more money.

- *The feeling that someone has your back*
  I provide for us. No one provides for me. Period.

- *Buying things for myself that I have rightfully earned and deserve*
  The number of times I've tried to squirrel away funds over a period of months to save for something dear to me—only to have it taken in full by an unexpected home expense—is many. Like the time I entertained buying myself a gorgeous platinum ring with diamonds that formed the shape of flowers but was brought right back into reality by a roof leak that demanded

repair. It devastates me every time. It's *my* money. I deserve nice things sometimes. Everyone does.

- ***The privilege of not always looking ahead to see what is coming***
  I've needed a break for a long time—a stretch of time where I'm not responsible for us or just responsible for me. It's hard to be still. When I'm quiet, all I think of is the noise our twenty-year-old furnace is making and how we will pay for a new one when it goes. The thought of another payment plan for something our house needs is heavy.

- ***Being a passenger***
  In life and in our car, I'm forever the driver. Forever in charge. I don't want to be. I want to zone out as someone else navigates traffic and finds parking. I want to look at a problem and say, "Let me know how that works out" instead of having to solve it.

Sympathy

Sympathy is a strange bird. It's an honest first reaction freely given by all to my disabled spouse. People meet him, immediately like him, and can't picture themselves doing what he does to get through life. The result is that he is showered with an overwhelming amount of admiration. He is well cared for by our friends. Every move he makes is praiseworthy. Do his clothes match? *He's amazing.* Did he vacuum our floor? *Wow, incredible.* Does he go into our local market and come out with a cake? *What an absolute hero.* And he is all of these things.

The underbelly of the admiration is that people generally have no expectations of him. They expect him not to function, and, so, if he functions minimally, they are in awe. But I'm not in awe. I believe in him. I know what he is capable of figuring out. I've seen him solve the most complicated challenges life has to offer. I'm not impressed that he can put on pants, clean the house, or figure out a way to buy things at our local market. This is a basic level of functioning and adaptation that anyone who has chosen to live a full life would figure out.

I love my husband, but there have been long spans of time when he has opted not to try. When he has been lazy at life. When he has wasted years. His life is hard, so, at times, he has chosen to take the equivalent of a "life nap" rather than rise to the challenge. But, then again, why would he take on something truly challenging when he was constantly being showered with praise for putting on pants?

You know who *doesn't* get sympathy? Spouses of disabled people. Maybe people look at me and think, *She knew what she was getting into. What did she expect?* But I didn't know what to expect. I'd never been married before and certainly not to a blind man. He was just figuring out blindness himself, so how was *I* supposed to have it figured out? This life is one that you live as it unfolds. And one thing you figure out is that disability absolutely makes life harder. It dismantles pieces of the life you are trying hard to build. Along the way, we, as spouses, give up a lot of our own dreams. We go without. We hold down the fort. We are the strong shoulder, the listening ear, the easy target for their frustration. We do a lot, and we are so freaking tired. *We* want the opportunity to take a "life nap," too. But then, who would pay the mortgage? And, maybe more importantly, who would buy the pants our spouses get praised to put on?

Do It Yourself

In our small town, there are two local takeout places that we order from quite a bit. When we go there, I send Joe in to pick up the food while I wait in the car. He knows these routes. He knows the cashiers. When he comes back to the car with the food, he is often accompanied by the cashiers, who want to make sure he gets back to the car safely. To the untrained eye, I look like a terrible wife—sending my blind spouse in to get food when I'm the one with vision. I don't care. What they don't see is that I work all day. I'm up three hours before him, getting the work of our household done before going to my real job. I manage our lives. I pay the bills. I stretch the money. I do all the things. At day's end, picking up a takeout order is something he can do. It gives me a ten-minute break. I deserve that. If it takes well-meaning cashiers and total strangers walking him back to our car (he can get there without them . . . they just feel bad) to give me a break, to let me experience being cared for, so be it. I can only smile at the confused looks I catch as they see me happily distracted on my phone while he tries to find the door handle.

MONEY

As we got older, the challenges we faced because of blindness hurt more. Friends who had started out as broke as us became established in their careers. They made more money and left behind the financial scrambling that makes up your twenties, but we never left that behind. I have had the good fortune of consistent work, but Joe has not. For the entirety of our twenty-eight-plus years (as of this writing) marriage, I have worked full-time. Joe has not. There have been years when he was enrolled in school, a short period of full-time work, and then part-time work as his vision faded and he needed a new career. There have been massive spans of time when he didn't work at all and times where he worked eight hours/week.

Maybe others would have figured out a sustainable career early on and focused on that. He did not. His approach was always to work doing things he loved for as long as he could. Then, when the vision loss demanded it, he would change to something brand new and do that for as long as he could. Each job change was like starting a new career, complete with the entry-level pay rate. Over the course of our marriage, he has been a bike-shop mechanic, an optician (nope, that's not a typo), a mailroom clerk, a luthier (another name for guitar builder), and a music-group leader. Each career was a starting over. So, as our friends became older and financially stable, we became older and financially no different than we were when we started out.

When we were in our twenties, a big budget "item" would be a night out to the movies with dinner. That changed as we got older. By the time we hit our fifties, all around us, friends were paying off their homes, traveling, and purchasing new cars or the latest technology. That was not to be for us. We have our home, and it will be paid off probably about twenty-four hours before I retire—and I can retire probably about twenty-four hours before I die. Our mode of transportation for many years of our marriage was a twenty-year-old Camry (Toyotas are amazing). Any vacations we planned were painstakingly budgeted. I put away for retirement. He lived off of disability payments and part-time work. We didn't have savings. Well, we did, but then emergencies happened that wiped that account clean. Juggling expenses was not fun. If you've ever, as I have, put off a root canal for six weeks to ensure that your FSA funds would kick in and cover it, you know what I mean. If you've ever tried to balance multiple payment plans for non-negotiable home repairs, you know what I mean, too. It was a struggle to maintain our home, and any debt we were in was because of it.

At one point, we dug ourselves out of almost $30k in credit-card debt. That hurts to even write. How does that happen? It's easy, actually. That happens when you live a life you can't afford, even if it's not extravagant. House maintenance is not for the weak or the broke. We were constantly fixing our home back then, and we justified our charged Home Depot purchases as a good investment in the future. And the repairs kept coming. We had put off repaving our driveway for years, until the day came that it literally disintegrated beneath us, requiring $7,000 we did not have. At one point, we thought about selling our home and moving into a condo, because low-maintenance condo life sounded like a nice next step. We updated our kitchen, redid the floors, and renovated the basement, certain that any updates we made to the house would make us a nice profit when we sold. But the more we updated the house, the more we liked it. We liked it so much, in fact, that we decided not to sell at all. So, our plan to recoup the investment into the house was a bit of a bust.

Living with debt was suffocating. We knew we had to take control of it. There are probably many good ways to tackle debt, but the one that worked for us was to take out a low-interest loan through our credit union and use that to pay off our high-interest credit card. It helped to have one predictable monthly payment and an actual end date for when the debt would be gone. Most importantly, we had to stop using our credit card. This was hard. We watched a lot of life go by. We didn't go on vacations. We stopped shopping for new clothes and became secondhand-store fans. We tried not to want things.

I would be lying if I said it didn't hurt to be around people who were living well on two solid incomes. It hurt to be working so hard while always knowing in the back of my mind that one more emergency expense could topple us over.

This was the life I didn't see coming when I was seventeen. I was focused only on the happy life we would have with each other. I overestimated his future ability to contribute financially, and I underestimated my own desire for a financially stable life. Turns out, I really quite like the thought of having enough income to easily go on vacation, spend money on hobbies, or go out to eat whenever I like. I always thought he would work full-time because he was working full-time when I met him. I thought a lot about the things he would have to give up as a blind person. But I never thought of all the things *I would* have to give up.

I saw the money that came in and the money that had to go out each month. I saw the expected bills and the unexpected expenses. I saw the fun things we couldn't do. I saw the worthy expenses line up and had to pick which ones got priority. It was heavy.

I've never bought into the model of marriage where the man is the provider. That has always seemed like an unfair expectation to place on any one person's shoulders. I never expected to be provided for. I've always known that I'd need to work hard to get what I need in life.

Yet, I also never wanted to be the main breadwinner. I thought we'd be an equal team. I grew up in and around families in which both parents worked, so that's what I was expecting. I never anticipated that I would be providing for us both. Maybe I should have.

Go Fund Me

The generosity of those around us along the way has proven to be a beautiful buffer to the harder parts of this life. Sometimes it's complicated, though. For example, Joe had once been a skilled woodworker but gave it up and sold all of his tools when he lost his vision. A few years ago, a great friend of ours set up a Go Fund Me page to help him re-purchase some tools so he could experiment with woodworking again as a blind person. Money came in pretty quickly, which enabled him to repopulate his shop with tools. Amazing, right? I love our friends and that they are this kindhearted toward him. I love that they believed in him that much. But I was torn by this offering. In my opinion, Go Fund Me was for people who had exhausted their own resources after trying as hard as they could. It was for people to cover basic expenses while they cared for a loved one during, say, cancer treatment. At that point, the Joe I spent my days with wasn't trying all that hard at life. Here he sat, working three hours a week, not looking hard for more work, letting people give him money for tools. The Go Fund Me page was a kindhearted offering, but my only thought was *Why should others give their hard-earned money to someone who wasn't even breaking a sweat trying to help himself?* I found it embarrassing. Joe thought it was great.

Maybe it was both. I'm over here stretching our monthly budget to make sure our bills were paid, leaving nothing extra for me to pursue my dreams while he sits still and watches a magical pot of money appear specifically for him to pursue his dreams. *Little shit.* Such is life.

HOW TIME CHANGES THINGS

Early on, I thought about disability from a safe distance. It was neat and almost contained. My husband didn't drive, and we worked around that. Blindness didn't impact me beyond that.

As years passed, the impact of blindness became more pronounced. It's so much more complicated than just arranging rides for someone not able to drive. It is bittersweet to walk together through the same world and see it differently. Even walking our dog at the local trail is a different experience for us. While Joe naturally relaxes into peaceful conversation during our walks, I'm constantly scanning the ground for obstacles, the woods for coyotes, and oncoming dog owners to see if their dog is leashed so that it doesn't interfere with mine. I love seeing, but my experience is never as peaceful as his because we are taking in different information. I miss both of us taking in the same information. I miss splitting the burden and deciding what to do about the things we see in the world. I wish I had help for the mundane things that fill up life, like finding a parking spot or figuring out which concert parking lot is the smartest one to pull into if we don't want to be stuck for three hours trying to exit after a show. It's a strange adjustment to live with someone who does not see the world around him, who does not even see *me*.

There were days I wished for more. I love my husband, but sometimes I saw the life that could have been mine, and it hurt.

The Girl I Could Have Been

Sometimes
I catch glimpses of her
In pictures
The girl I could have been

Not distracted by disability

Paired with a true partner
An equal contributor

Well cared for
Well loved

Untethered to heartache
Steadily moving
Toward her dreams

Dreams known well
And supported fully
By those most important to her

Living happily
Not always carrying
The weight
Of the world
Of his world
In particular

I see her sometimes
She looks so free

And I wish
That I was
Too

None of the early ideas I had about how blindness would eventually impact our lives took into account disability limiting us in any way. Because Joe had always been so steady and positive in his approach to living with blindness, I thought it would always be this way. I sincerely thought that physical disability wouldn't change us. Wouldn't ever feel like a burden to me or an impossible mountain to him. I see now that my words and thoughts lacked the wisdom that can come only from experience. I was young and didn't account for or allow for our humanity.

I used to approach any deep pain that life threw my way with open arms, almost grateful to be entrusted with such a challenge. I never complained about Joe's blindness or let myself be angry that this was happening to someone I love. I believed that painful things happened for a reason. I believed we could get through anything. My earliest poems reflect this optimism.

Weep

You will see me weep
You will catch me in different seasons of loss
You will see me break down at the thought of the one I love breaking down
You will see me grieve each time I see something beautiful and can't share it with the one with whom I share all things
You will hear angry words in moments of despair
You will see that I don't handle multiple losses very well

But this you need to know
Know that God has been good to us
Know that we are blessed
Know that if this is God's will for us
we would have it no other way
Know that these tears of sadness are not bitter tears

Know that accepting the idea of blindness is easier
than accepting the daily realities that go with it

Know these things
and you will know how this broken heart has peace

The realities of blindness changed how I view life. I don't believe that things happen for a reason anymore. Though I do believe that pain is a normal and random part of every one of our lives, I no longer believe that God sends the pain for some higher purpose. When devastation enters my life now, I don't feel pressure to find it acceptable. I allow myself to *feel all the feelings*. To rage. To cry. To complain. To be human.

I embrace the girl who wrote so honestly during early blindness, even if I no longer agree with her.

I love who she was and the hope she carried for so long.

I also love that I know so much more now.

Mostly, I know now that it's possible to love a person but to wish things were easier.

There were definitely some very painful days as Joe's vision declined. I remember feeling sad but not devasted on the day he told me that he could no longer see the yellow highlighting on a document that was in front of him. I remember feeling like curling up in a ball the day he told me that he could no longer see stars. I remember feeling guilty soon after, as I looked up into the night sky and saw what he would never see again. We mourned these losses individually, in pieces, while trying to brace ourselves for the day he would no longer see anything. I pictured that day in the far-off future. I pictured him waking up and telling me he no longer had any vision. I pictured it as a quiet, somber—but not hopeless—day. I pictured me calling into work and us spending the day together just acknowledging and honoring the end of vision. Sounds so peaceful and mature, doesn't it?

I May Call In That Day

I may call in that day
When you wake up
And open your eyes
To darkness

Take the day off
To be beside you
To shed a tear
To feel the brokenness

To mark an end
To mark a beginning
To welcome this new chapter
In our lives

And in case you forget
To remind you of the things
That blindness
Just can't touch

The essence of you
The things you have accomplished
The lives you have touched
The challenges you have overcome

Your natural curiosity
Your history of doing the impossible
Your passion for music
Your passion for life

The way you so effortlessly crack people up
The way you contribute heavily to this world

How Time Changes Things

The rich, full life that awaits you
The amazing plan that God has for you

I may call in that day
When you wake up

And open your eyes
To darkness

If only to share with you this moment
Of knowing without a doubt
That our God is about to guide us

Through the best days of our lives

As it turns out, accepting blindness wasn't quite as easy as calling into work and being together on the day blindness hit. It wasn't that easy at all. Blindness like this doesn't just "hit" one day. It's more of a cumulative build. You can't predict the impact. You can experience it only as it unfolds. It was against the backdrop of blindness that mental-health issues arrived.

Section II

Mental Health

HOW IT STARTED

Blindness was an expected disability. It hung like a dark cloud in the distance, creeping closer every day—but, at least, we knew the storm was coming. Though we could never accurately envision the day-to-day details of what living blind would mean, at least we had some time to accept the idea that blindness would be part of our lives.

The arrival of mental-health issues was entirely unexpected. They entered our lives fifteen years into our marriage, and we were decidedly not prepared for them. They came in with such devastation that they made blindness look laughable.

Mental-health issues changed every single thing about our lives. I don't know that words even exist to fully describe the impact.

What I can say is that, out of the blue and over a very short period of time, my husband became delusional. The police came to our home, and, after a very ugly struggle, he was transported to the hospital for evaluation. This began a turbulent period that included multiple hospitalizations for psychosis and suicidality as well as many years of deep depression. The road back was steep, cold, and cruel, but we made it.

And when I look at the description written that way, the way most people are comfortable with hearing it, I can see why people don't fully understand how life-changing this was. Let me try again with different words.

Over a period of about two weeks—before the morning I had no choice but to call the police to our home to subdue my psychotic husband—he had become fixated with talking about the Catholic Church, the Pope, and religion in general. At every opportunity, he talked incessantly about the Bible and how, though it was confusing, he was beginning to understand it and felt like he was being given special insight into what it all meant. I remember being annoyed by his insistence on talking about these topics and how it was hard to shut him up. On Halloween, as we were giving out candy, I remember being frustrated that, even on that night, he wouldn't stop talking. Oftentimes, he would talk in circles, never quite getting to a point—but he thought he was making perfect sense.

The day before he was hospitalized, his energy became wild and unpredictable. By that point, he hadn't slept for three days. He had a fever and bronchitis. His words started to sound like paranoia. At times, his voice got loud, and his words became nonsensical. At one point, he tried to block my exit from a room. In the middle of the night, I found him standing motionless in our bathroom, asking for my permission to move. He was so confused and scared. I was also confused and scared. After several nonstop hours of me trying to manage his intensity, he became threatening. In our entire fifteen years of marriage up until that time, my husband had been a mild-mannered, peaceful person who rarely said an unkind word to or about anyone. But that morning, his wild energy reached a peak: he was standing inches away from my face, screaming horrible words and threatening to hit me. I ran out of my house and got the police.

Overall, that might not seem like much to some people. After all, he didn't hit me. And mean words are just words. But that morning changed everything. Blew up whatever peaceful history we had enjoyed. Changed us from a happy, easygoing couple to strangers existing in separate worlds. The old versions of us died that day, because, that morning, a new and unwelcomed element was introduced into our marriage—terror. The person who had caused my terror was going to need an impossible amount of help to get better. He would need help from many, but, specifically, he would require a lot of help from *me.* So I shoved the impact of all that had happened down deep, because I had to deal with his brokenness first. Later, I would deal with mine.

I hate writing the details of those hours just before Joe was hospitalized. I actually wonder if I should leave this much information in. I wonder if it will make people judge Joe forever or if this is exactly what's needed to show people how alarming the actions of people in the depths of illness can be. This is why walking the road of mental illness is so isolating. Asking others who aren't living the experience firsthand to hold truths that I myself—the person who *did* actually live it—have trouble holding is likely asking too much. I leave these details in because I want other people going through a similar hell to know that the trauma they experienced *matters.* And if the details of their own hell are still too sensitive to share with their own loved ones, maybe they could share mine instead and say, "It's kind of like this."

But back to that morning.

I got out of my house. When the police came, Joe assaulted them. His brain had convinced him that anyone coming to help him was really there to hurt him, and so he acted accordingly. He was taken, naked and restrained on a gurney, to the local hospital. He was screaming as they loaded him into the ambulance. This was his first-ever hospitalization, but it would be one of four admissions that year.

I never knew someone could change so quickly. Didn't think it was even a possibility. That awful morning, I realized in an instant that the husband I had known so well had ceased to exist. It was devastating.

Months later, when his brain healed a bit, he was no longer psychotic or delusional—but acutely suicidal. For many years, we lived this way, on the edge of death and hopelessness. Our happy marriage was over. I gave everything I had to keep him engaged in treatment. He gave me nothing in return—not a smile, not a word of kindness. Everything I knew about him, God, and myself disintegrated. After four pretty-solid years of hell, small improvements began to show themselves. And by "small," I mean like the day he put a filter in the coffee pot and made coffee. That act was a monumental demonstration of engagement with life for him. Somehow, we made it to the other side. We rebuilt our lives and healed our minds and souls.

That's what happened. Or maybe I should say, *That was the beginning of what happened and started us on a long path into and through mental illness.* And that description—that level of truth and vulnerability—feels a little more honest. I know it's the right level of vulnerability when I cringe a bit at what I am sharing and wonder how it will be received and when it's clear that the truth of what I lived through might make some people want to look away rather than keep reading. That is the level of transparency I am aiming for. I hope you won't look away.

Blindness is a physical disability with a specific cause, a specific thing to blame. His eyes don't work. That's why he is blind. Period.

Mental illness is mysterious, scary, and laden with shame. Others look on from the outside and think: *Why did his brain break? What exactly happened? What's wrong with him? His behavior is confusing, so I'm going to keep my distance. He isn't being the friend that he used to be to me, so I am going to cut him loose.*

Brain problems make people run in the other direction. I get it.

I didn't sign up for a marriage that would give me nothing in return. Leaving was *always* an option. But leaving soon after the initial mental-health event was not even on my radar, in the same way that leaving someone right after they've been in a life-altering car wreck isn't usually top of mind.

Recovery—be it physical or mental—can take an excruciatingly long time. Many in our lives couldn't stick around for it.

I watched a lot of people leave surprisingly early in the recovery process—possibly because they didn't think he would recover.

And secretly, I flipped every one of them the bird as they walked away.

Watched Your Life Change

Have you ever
Watched your life change

Before your eyes

Saw in slow motion
Everything important
Fall away

Reached out hands
In a frantic attempt
To grab some pieces
Before they were gone

And come up empty

Have you ever
Watched your life change

Watched everything familiar
Sink into a hole
Taking with it
The map
For your life

Have you ever
Watched your life change

Known instantly
Nothing more
Could be done
To save it

How It Started

Known only
The life
Left behind
Was staring you
In the face

Asking the impossible
Still needing
To be lived

My Life Ended That Day

My life ended that day
The day you heard about
The day your heart broke upon the hearing
The day long since forgotten by many

And rightly so
It's not anyone else's battle
But my own

A distant memory for most
So much time has passed
Time spent by some
Traveling to new places
Smelling the flowers
Making memories with loved ones

But my life ended that day
And since that day
There have been no vacations
No smelling of flowers
No peaceful time with loved ones

Just a long, hard journey
To find life again
And figure out
How to live it

BACK TO SHITTY

Now that I've shared a high-level view of what happened that morning, it's hard to know where to dive into the story that follows. Do I start with how mental illness impacted our marriage? Do I start with how hard it was to find the right therapists and prescribers? Do I start with how spectacularly broken the mental-health system proved itself to be? Do I start with how our friendships changed because of it? Do I start with how deep the grief that followed was?

For the sake of clarity, I think this part of the story is best told in snapshots. Recovery from mental-health issues is a winding road filled with stops and starts, progress and relapse, hope and despair. Any attempt to share it chronologically would only give you whiplash. I want to avoid that because I care deeply about your neck.

I also want to strike a balance between being brutally honest about how life was while acknowledging that it's impossible to share it all or share it perfectly. So with the belief that imperfectly shared stories are still worth telling, I'll start by sharing the stories that give the clearest glimpse into what our lives looked like the first few years.

Early on in mental-health issues, when people asked how it was going, I used to say, "We have a long way to go just to get our lives back to shitty"—meaning just to get our lives back to simply going blind, back to just figuring out how to manage our old mundane

"How are we going to balance this budget?" and "Let's make a plan to eat healthier—here, have some kale" day-to-day life. The addition of a mental-health crisis to our lives marked the beginning of a very long lonely road. I wish I could say that, after the initial crisis hospitalization, we figured out clear next steps for healing and quickly saw improvement, but that's not how it worked. That's not actually how mental-health issues work. Treatment plans and diagnosis around mental-health conditions aren't clear-cut. The road to mental wellness is incredibly difficult and discouraging and often goes in circles for a long while before a path opens up that leads you home. I would have given anything for a normal shitty life back then rather than the "Oh, look—the outhouse seems to have tipped over and now we are drowning in it" life that had become our reality.

Ebb and Flow

Nothing is easy with mental-health recovery. Every day you give all you have, and every day you give up.

Every time a new medicine was prescribed, I had a burst of hope that this might be the one that helped Joe make progress. Every time he came out of therapy and shared something insightful that he had learned, I thought to myself, *Now he is on the road to healing, and I can exhale.* These moments of hope were offset every time he had to be taken off of a medication due to side effects or ineffectiveness and every time he came out of therapy as hopeless as when he'd gone in.

Recovery is circular, and, just at the point where you think you can see improvement and envision a happy future life, you are pulled backwards into the abyss. Eventually something gets better and stays better. Then another thing. And then—look at that: another! There comes a point where you start to let yourself believe that it might someday be okay or at least okay-ish. A day when you find yourself looking out into the future with a cautious hope. Not unlike the way you might look out over a mile of murky, alligator-infested waters and see what looks like a peaceful shore in the distance, knowing it's going to be a hell of a swim, and, even if you do make it to the other side, some important parts of you might be missing.

After that initial morning when Joe was first hospitalized, my Mom stayed with me, magically appearing before me with encouraging words and bowls of cut-up fruit. She cleaned my house to within an inch of its life while I went back and forth between sitting silently and scouring the internet for information about mental-health issues. When she left, I moved into my brother's house for a few weeks, too distraught to think straight or figure out how to be alone. It wasn't aloneness that I feared actually. I'm a loner by nature. It was being alone in a house where bad memories had just been made.

Before this happened to us, I didn't know anything about mental-health recovery. I thought that it would be like recovery from a physical injury. Kind of like when you fall and need stitches, that first day is usually the worst, but, once stitched up, things get better because our bodies naturally go toward healing. I learned that healing a brain is a little more complicated. The day of Joe's break was certainly the worst, but, even after hospital treatment, he had days of reverse progress. Despite the fact that he was in active treatment and never missed his weekly outpatient-therapy appointments, he was re-hospitalized several times. I felt incredibly helpless sacrificing all of the money, time, and energy I had to ensure he had access to the right therapists and psychiatrists, only to realize even *that* didn't seem to be enough to keep him well. I found hope very hard to maintain. It took years of practice for me to get used to the ebb and flow of how mental-health recovery goes, if it goes at all.

Day Filling

The first time that Joe got admitted to the hospital, I thought that he wouldn't be released until he was well. I was wrong. I learned that the true wellness journey would begin only once he was released and linked with the right long-term providers. I learned that the space between crisis and wellness is a dense and dangerous wilderness. Joe's thoughts and speech continued to be confusing and concerning even after his release from the hospital. I felt alone, extremely aggravated, and more than a little exhausted. I wanted to scream, "Is this the best we can do for a good human who just had a mental-health issue unexpectedly dropped on him?" If Joe had been home speaking in an unorganized way due to stroke, he would have been whisked off and admitted as a priority to the hospital until stabilized. But because mental-health issues were the cause of the confused speech, most of the recovery was done at home. I found it traumatizing to witness Joe's confusion. If there is a handbook for how best to live with someone recovering from paranoia and delusion, I can only imagine it says something like "Welcome to Hell. Don't take anything to heart. Fight the fear and sadness you feel, or it will swallow you whole. Also, try to stay hydrated. That part won't help a bit, but it's the only part of this advice that's doable."

After each inpatient hospitalization came a two-week outpatient hospitalization (day program) to help him ease back into life. So during the day, he attended a program, and, at night, he came home. Once that was done, there was nothing. He was home with no job to go to, no structure to his days, and endless hours to let thoughts about his terrible life take root and grow. Other than a few weekly one-hour therapy/psychiatry appointments, there was simply nothingness; a very dangerous scenario for anyone struggling with suicidal thoughts. We were in dire need of ideas for filling up his days. At first, the plan was to have friends and family come and be with him while I went back to work. Yet no matter how loved a person is, it's not possible to have unpaid 24/7 coverage for another human. Most of his time was spent alone. Predictably, he spiraled and was re-hospitalized several times. Though every hospitalization was devastating, it bought us time. When he was in the hospital, he was "safe," which meant that I could rest, and I could use the time to look for any activity that might be able to fill Joe's time when he got out. There were some "clubhouse" type day programs in our area, but they were targeted for people with intellectual disabilities rather than recovery from depression, mania, and psychosis. Tempting as it was to send him there just so he would not be alone during the day, I knew this would only make him feel more desperate.

With the "clubhouse" option ruled out, I turned my attention toward hobby clubs. Joe had loved woodworking and music before his break. Just before mental-health issues appeared, he was building guitars and teaching people how to build their own guitars out of our home workshop. But that option was now gone. With blindness seemingly taking everything good from him, I thought that linking him with others who shared his interests would give him a chance to meet new people with whom he had something in common and build new skills. This would have been a great plan if he'd been at all interested in meeting new people or building new skills. Turns out, he was not interested in any of that.

Tools

After a zillion Google searches that involved combinations such as "Blindness and Woodworking" and "Can blind people still use workshop tools?" I remember being so very proud of myself when I tracked down a unicorn of a human who specialized in teaching woodworking to blind people. I was beyond thrilled when he said he'd actually come to the house to meet with Joe. Before he came, I did more research and ordered a couple of the latest tools for blind woodworkers (e.g., a talking tape measure and something called a click rule to help fine-tune measurements). During those weeks, the Massachusetts Commission for the Blind even came out and gave Joe a new laptop, complete with the JAWS reader program, a very popular and very expensive "all the blind people are using this to communicate" kind of software installed.

By all accounts, Joe had what he needed to move forward.

Except that he didn't.

What he had was gadgets. What he did not have was hope. When the woodworking teacher came to our home and told us all of the exciting workarounds that enabled blind people to continue woodworking, Joe sat hunched over barely lifting his head. He was not impressed with or interested in the options before him. The part that Joe had liked most about woodworking was seeing the beauty of the wood, and, because he could no longer see the wood, he wanted no part of it. He was acutely depressed. He was also acutely rude. I was embarrassed. I was also quite aggravated because humans that teach woodworking to blind people aren't easy to find. As the man left, he pulled me aside and said, "Maybe this isn't a good idea right now," and I agreed. He walked away, taking with him any shred of hope that I had.

The laptop that Joe had been given also sat idle. The JAWS reader software installed on the computer was not intuitive, and this only added to Joe's sense of failure and overwhelm. Joe was not interested in woodworking. Joe was not interested in learning adaptive technology. More accurately, Joe was not interested in anything. But I was very interested in making Joe interested in anything at all, so I continued to look for options.

Later that year, I saw a news story about a local man who had lost his vision as an adult and was now climbing all the mountains in New Hampshire. I emailed him immediately (thank you, Google), and, to my surprise, he emailed back. We set up a time to meet for coffee with him and his wife in New Hampshire. What an amazing man, yes, but also what a nice couple. I remember that, on that day, they sat with us and listened and offered hope. They empathized about the challenges of navigating the early stages of blindness in a way that only those who have been through it can do. Sitting across from a man who had gone blind and was now living a happy life gave me hope again. I didn't know how Joe would be able to get from the state he was in that day to living a life of happiness and hope, but I did know it was possible. Was Joe perky during this visit? No. But on the way home, he turned to me and said, "I think that guy just changed my life." I wish I could say we got home and there were immediate signs of hope oozing from Joe, but there were not. Hopelessness was his constant companion for a very long time. Still, that he was able to appreciate meeting another person who was navigating blindness was a good sign.

How It Goes

Healing from a mental-health crisis is slow. Most days, it is hard to feel like any progress is being made. It's hard to hold out hope that life will ever get better.

Several months after the initial crisis, Joe was home but still nowhere near well. His mental health was tenuous. I had never lived with anyone experiencing depression, so the dark energy in our home was new to me. Joe usually stayed in bed or on the couch most of the day. Every day was pretty bad. I remember sitting at my desk, working from home one of those days. That day, instead of being in bed or on the couch, he opted to sit hopelessly behind me in a reclining chair. The actual air felt suffocating to me. Felt laden with the sadness he was not verbalizing; felt hopeless with the tears he was not crying. He had been hopeless for a while, but, that day, it got bad enough that he asked to go back into the hospital. He wanted to die. The ER staff believed him. He was admitted. Another week in the hospital, another two-week step-down day program afterwards. Another back at home trying desperately to figure out ways to keep him well.

Eleven months after the initial crisis, just as I arrived at work at 7:30 a.m. and was about to begin my day, my phone rang, and it was Joe. He said simply that he was not okay and needed to go to the hospital. I asked if he thought he would be safe for the 40 minutes it would take me to drive home and he said, "Yes." It's hard to know what's true in these situations. It's hard to know when you should call an ambulance or when you should trust that your person is able to keep himself safe. I kept him on the phone for a few minutes while I walked out of my office and gave him a task that I knew would distract him for a few minutes—the task of packing up a few outfits for the hospital. By that time, he had a favorite "hospital sweatshirt," which is a testament to the sad state of affairs that our life had become. I knew it would take him a while to locate that and put it in an overnight bag.

As I walked to my car, I called the hospital I knew I wanted him to be admitted to. I asked if they had open beds (they did) and then asked which ER we needed to go to in order to get him into one of those beds. So by the time I pulled into the driveway at home and gathered Joe, I knew exactly which ER had admitting rights to the psychiatric hospital I wanted him to be at, and that's where we headed. It's a fun fact that the ERs—which have to rule out medical issues first—are often at different locations than the psychiatric hospitals people end up at.

The hours spent in that ER were devastating, not just because it was yet another hospitalization but because of the convoluted conversations I endured while with him. He was paranoid and didn't feel safe in the care of the hospital staff. It would be eight hours before he was medically cleared for admission to the psychiatric ward a few towns over. By that point, he was terrified even to go into the ambulance for transport. The only way he would go is if I promised to drive right behind the ambulance the entire way and never lose sight of him. Of course, this was an impossibility, but I hatched a plan and slipped out of the room to talk to the paramedics who would be transporting him. When I explained how afraid my husband was at that moment, they offered to tilt the ambulance bed up so Joe would feel like I could see him through the back window. I told them the color and make of my car so that when Joe asked, they could easily confirm that, yes, there was a silver Camry right behind them the whole way. I look back on this idea and think, *Wow, Becky—that was such a creative and smart solution to getting him where he needed to be.* But I also think back on this time with tears. I was so exhausted. Every day required so much of me. I had to be clever. I didn't want to be clever. I just wanted my husband back. I felt like if I wasn't always ten steps ahead, he might not make it. I don't know if that was true. I do know that it was an unbearable burden to feel like if I stopped and rested—for even a second—no one else was going to do what needed to be done to help him.

It is traumatic to witness the person you love unravel. It's traumatic to witness mental anguish, to see such a deep level of suffering and not be able to do a thing about it other than stay there.

Another few weeks in the hospital.

Another two-week step-down day program.

Another back at home trying desperately to figure out ways to keep him well.

Rinse and repeat.
This was our life that first year.
Any other plans we may have had faded away.
Survival was the only goal.

Phone Bills and Calls

The amount of time I spent on the phone with hospitals, insurance companies, therapists, psychiatrists, and day programs trying to arrange care and next steps and services was immense. It took everything out of me. I'm not a phone person. I don't like talking to people. So the $600 cell-phone bill that came my way at the start of this crisis was witness to how much my life had changed. And yes, I did pick up the very phone I had grown to hate yet again to beg my cell-phone carrier for mercy, which they gave me by cutting that first bill in half. And, yes, all these years later, now that Joe is better, I never answer the phone anymore, because, after years of arranging shit, I am all talked out.

Program

It took months, but, eventually, I found a blind day program about an hour from our home called the "Lowell Association for the Blind" (LAB) that met twice each week and was free. The activities offered included everything from catered breakfasts, to bowling, lunch outings and apple picking. While everyone who attended was in different stages of vision loss, the common denominator was blindness. When I told Joe about this program, he agreed to attend one activity, and I agreed to attend with him. I remember the day so well. It was Valentine's Day, and the program was having a Valentine's Day party. The invitation said to bring a dessert, so I got busy making something called "Oreo Crack Balls" which was always a crowd pleaser. I remember walking into the party room that day and being greeted by such a positive group of blind people. They could not have been more friendly. Joe and I sat down at the table, and, as I made small talk with people nearby, I could see Joe out of the corner of my eye, disengaged, head slumped down, refusing to interact. He was in full *Weekend At Bernie's* mode, a lifeless body being dragged to places he didn't want to be and propped up for show. I was not happy with him. The effort it took me to find this program, the time I was taking off work to attend this first session with him—to have him not even try to *try* was infuriating. I was again embarrassed. Who was this arsehole of a husband by my side? He appreciated nothing that anyone did for him. The group was nice to him despite him. Plus they loved my Oreo balls. So, I decided, yes, this is where he will come twice a week, like it or not.

Canes, Trains, and Busses

Getting him to this program was another challenge altogether. *How do you get a depressed blind person to a program an hour away,* you might ask? In pieces. Our small town does not have public transportation, and, as a result, there is a shuttle service that will pick up residents at their homes and drive them to the nearest train station. From the train station, Joe would then need to board a bus, get off at the correct stop, cross a busy street, and walk a few blocks to the entrance of the program. At this point in time, breathing overwhelmed Joe. As an example, during those days, I worked hard on coming up with simple ideas to get him out of bed and engaged with life in its most basic form. I once enlisted him to help me make a ridiculously easy Crockpot chili recipe, and his role was simply to open a few cans of beans and dump them into the Crockpot.

I remember him standing there, can opener in hand, head tilted my way, saying "This is so hard." This is the level of "umph" his depression was allowing him to muster. So the thought of him getting on a shuttle and then a bus to get to where he needed to be was not promising. I knew he would not do it alone.

I remember asking my boss—with all of two days' notice—if I could be home for a few weeks so I could practice going back and forth to the program with Joe. Thankfully this request was approved, and, for the next two weeks, I worked from home until noon and then spent the afternoons helping Joe learn the route. We quite literally practiced taking the shuttle to the train station, finding the correct bus, walking to the program, and then turning around and doing the same route in reverse. It was not easy. Depressed as he was, Joe agreed to do what it took to get to the program. If he opted out of this program, there was no other plan. If he could get to this program, it would give him something to do two days a week while he recovered.

It took a few months, but, eventually, Joe learned to like the program and enjoy the people in the group. They broke him down with their kindness and had zero expectations of him. They didn't know the old, super-high-functioning version of Joe, so they were not disappointed with the depressed version of him. They didn't know the Joe who used to make everyone around him feel loved and seen. They didn't know the Joe that would have people doubled over in laughter with his jokes. They didn't know the Joe who used to show up to life guitar in hand and be leading all in a sing-a-long before they ever knew what hit them. The Joe that attended this program had nothing to offer. He showed up as his current broken self and was accepted. What a gift. Every once in a while, I would go to activities with the group, too. Once I went bowling, and they broke up the teams into girls vs. guys. Yes, I did play on the girls' team and yes, I did lose to all of the other blind bowlers on my team. No, I don't want to talk about it. Please respect my privacy at this difficult time.

Struggle and Progress

What I'm trying to convey in this section is that there is no straight path to healing. From the outside looking in, it might have appeared that every progress made meant Joe was no longer struggling. But he struggled and made progress simultaneously. And we never knew if the progress would be enough or if the struggle would eventually win.

JAWS

The laptop that Joe had been given sat idle. The JAWS program that was installed on it was one of the most popular screen-reader programs for blind people. This program enables blind users to communicate with the sighted world by doing everything from reading emails and word documents out loud to verbally walking blind users through internet pages. JAWS is known for being challenging to learn, but it is such an important tool that blind users generally think it's worth the effort.

Joe's battle to learn JAWS was a scrappy, dirty, hard-fought battle to the death. He knew how important it was to master this program. He knew that JAWS was his link back to the world that blindness had taken away. But he found navigating JAWS extremely complicated. It's such an unusual way of getting information that I think of it as a different language. People do learn new languages all the time, but it usually does not include the added burden of knowing that your entire future quality of life hinges on how well the language is mastered. Despite his depressed state, Joe made several attempts to learn JAWS. But the trainings left him feeling overwhelmed rather than informed.

Early in Joe's depression, the Massachusetts Commission for the Blind (MCB) funded a three-week, full-time, live-in JAWS immersion training. After so many months of hopelessness and gloom, I was beyond excited that he was being given this opportunity. I was so very happy that he would be taught a new way not only to receive information but also share information with the world. I dropped Joe off at this program an hour away with a suitcase full of clothes and a heart full of hope that this could be exactly what was needed to help him start walking toward life again. The other reason this training was a source of happiness was that it gave me a three-week reprieve from caring for Joe. I don't say that to be mean. I say that because I was a caregiver who was running on empty and in desperate need of a break. The very thought of me having several weeks alone at home to care for myself while Joe received life-changing training was the biggest win-win scenario in the history of wins. I had three beautiful weeks to myself. I slept well. I cooked myself fun meals. I read late into the night. My home was light and happy—no sign of depression for miles. Joe did complete three solid weeks of JAWS training. But as it turns out, eight hours a day of complicated software training was not an effective format for Joe. JAWS software is complex to even the happiest of people, but, to the depressed mind, it seemed impossible. The whole experience discouraged Joe. I couldn't blame him for not thriving. I'd set my hair on fire if I had to sit through eight hours a day of any type of software training for three weeks.

Still, my heart sank into itself a bit more after this experience. The husband I picked up from this program three weeks later was even more depressed than the one I'd dropped off. I had hoped for a breakthrough but what I got was more brokenness. I know now that this is often how the climb back from mental-health issues goes. I was constantly trying to figure out solutions to make life lighter. But sometimes the steps that I was sure would make life lighter and better only made life harder and heavier. What I got back from that program was a more-exhausted, more-discouraged husband. And now he was dragging a full suitcase of dirty laundry behind him.

In order for Joe to move forward, many impossible circumstances would need to align. His depression would need to quiet down. He would need to be brave enough to try again. The training format would need to inspire curiosity and leave him believing that he could succeed versus push him to recede into himself. It seemed like a lot to ask.

Several months later, MCB funded another JAWS training for Joe. This was a two-week day-training format in Boston rather than a live-in immersion format. He could commute in and be home by dinner each night. Joe was still depressed but seemed a bit more hopeful. We both thought this opportunity could work. And once again, we were both wrong. The intensity of all-day JAWS trainings was still too much. He finished the training but was still unable to use JAWS.

I could feel pieces of me dying every time seemingly good opportunities were not good for Joe. I was getting used to having my hopes crushed. We both knew that conquering even the most basic parts of JAWS was the next required step for Joe, and, every time he tried and failed, we wondered if this was as far as he'd go in life. We wondered if this was as good as life was going to get. Life was pretty awful, so, if this was the new peak, it didn't seem like a life worth having. It was scary to have this complicated software program be the thing standing between Joe's painful present and his possible future. It's not like there were tons of options out there in the world for learning JAWS. Yes, standard trainings were available. But customized trainings for severely depressed blind people who don't want to be blind and aren't quite sure they want to live—those trainings weren't available.

When we eventually found the LAB/blind day program, my heart filled with hope once again when I learned that free 1:1 JAWS tutoring was available there from one of the women who also attended the day program. How wonderful to have focused training time with an instructor all to himself! This was exactly the approach that Joe needed. If you've read this far, you know that having all the right pieces in place does not guarantee progress. And that was the case once again. After a few sessions, despite the most ideal training format imaginable, Joe let me know that he still was not coming out of the sessions with useful information or tangible skills. It was devastating to realize that these trainings—either because of the depression, the content, or the training style—were not working for him. I knew Joe's brain was still healing from mental trauma, but I started to wonder if his brain was permanently broken. If classes didn't work and 1:1 training didn't work, would anything ever work?

Joe was living a pretty isolated life at this time. If he wasn't at therapy or the day program, he was home. He needed a way to re-engage with the world, and learning JAWS was the obvious next mountain to be climbed. Opportunities and trainings were continually dangled in front of him, but he couldn't maintain a grip on them. Despite the many external resources and supports, it was internal resources that he desperately needed, and he had zero. I had to remind myself to be thankful that he was attending the day program at all. At the very least, he was being exposed to other blind people who were managing to live somewhat happy lives. Even if he couldn't be one, he could not deny they existed.

Not too long after Joe had stopped attending the 1:1 JAWS training sessions, the blind day program announced that it was offering a radio-programming internship. This internship would teach the technical skills needed to run a radio program and also give opportunities to interview guests. For the first time in a long time, Joe's interest was piqued. I knew that getting this internship would be a real game changer for Joe's confidence. There was only one problem: Knowledge of JAWS was a non-negotiable requirement.

JAWS was the mountain we could not seem to climb over, get around, or push through. But we didn't want to live at the base of this mountain forever. What does one do when it seems like every option has been exhausted? Apparently, one Googles. Hours of searching for options led me to a highly recommended JAWS trainer who was willing to come to the house and work with Joe 1:1. She was a professional trainer who could customize sessions to Joe's learning needs. She seemed like just the right blend of compassion and knowledge. When she told me her rate, it felt like a gut punch, but if $175 an hour was what it would take to bring Joe back to life, then what choice did we really have? The plan was to schedule three initial sessions and see if this was the training that would help Joe move forward. When I called her to set up the first session, I learned that the quoted rate of $175 did not include an additional transportation fee of $75. So if $175/hour felt like a gut punch, $250/hour felt like a full-body wrecking ball. $250/hour was absurd, and I was out of tears by that point. I had no more money to give; I had no more of myself to give.

I wanted to give up. And as sometimes (but not always) happens when we are about to give up, someone unexpected stepped up at that very moment and handed me a check to cover three sessions in full. Someone gave us that money, no strings attached. Who would do this? After all, the struggle to get Joe training was a private battle that I hadn't shared freely. And the ups and downs of mental-health issues tend to drive people away, so our circle was small during those years. The person who gave us this check might best be described as an acquaintance. Someone watching from the sidelines who could see that it was almost *game over* and decided to jump in to give us more lives in the nick of time.

The 1:1 JAWS sessions, led by a professional trainer in our home, gave Joe the information he needed. At the end of his third session, he applied for and was awarded the radio-programming internship. He still had a long way to go to come back to life, but he was on his way.

Community College

After a few years of attending the blind day program, and experiencing some success using JAWS, Joe mustered up the courage to enroll in a local community college to work toward his associate degree in drug and alcohol counseling. At first, he took one class per semester. He had completed some college courses in the past but never as a blind person. Now he was linked with resources to help him succeed. He was assigned note-takers in his class, who documented key information and sent it to him to study. He also took tests in the disability office, with assistive devices. The staff at the disability center believed in him. It was a slow, steady climb. He gained momentum. By his last semester, he was taking multiple classes at a time and doing quite well. It was inspiring.

To most, it looked like the worst was over. But he still didn't want to live. He did what needed to be done at school, but most hours at home, he slept. When awake, he had the look of a person thinking heavy thoughts. He was distant—quiet but not in a reflective way. Quiet in the way a person gets silent when weighing whether or not they want to stay here. I learned then that people can go about their daily activities checking off all the boxes and still be suicidal, still be thinking every day of ways to die.

Miracles

Miracles are not
Snap your fingers and
Life is better
Sickness is healed
Happiness is restored

Miracles are
You are still alive
When you feel dead

Miracles are
One more idea
When the idea well is dry

Miracles are
Not dying from
Exhaustion or hopelessness

Miracles are
Having any shred of faith left
When all you have known
Is gone

Miracles are
A spark of hope
In the darkness of odds
That don't hold much promise

Miracles are
The single breath you get to take
When you burst to the surface for air
Just before going under again

Back to Shitty

Miracles are
Temporary relief from pain
A little company on a lonely road

Miracles are
Improving more than people thought
Doing better but not doing well
Being okay though okay is not whole

Miracles are
Small breaks of laughter
That tell the pain to
Go to hell

Miracles are
Monday picnics
Pretty skies and
Inspiring teabags

Miracles are
That anyone is left in your life
When you've spent them all up
With your pain

Miracles are
Different from happy endings
Or resolution
Or enough for the long haul

Miracles are
Nothing like
I thought
They were

Miracles are
A damn lot
Of work

Dread

This morning
All these months later
It occurred to me
That the first feeling
I have felt
Every morning
For the last
Fourteen months
When I wake up
Is dread
For the day ahead

A quick flash
Of a feeling
Before I get out of bed
And shake it off
And live the day

But that first feeling
When I think of
The day ahead
Is unmistakably
Dread

A feeling
That has become
So much part of me
So unconscious
So routine
I didn't even
Recognize it as odd

But today
I remembered
Mornings in the past
Waking up with hope
Anticipation
Looking forward
To what the day held
What life held

Sad that has left me

Sad I didn't realize
How much was gone
How deeply gone
Is my hope

Not even sure now
That dread is warranted
But it's there
Clear as day
Taking up the space
Where hope lived

Best I can do now
Is chip away
At the dread
Till it is no longer
Attached to my soul

Not looking for
Happy days just yet
Only the return
Of hope for
Happier days

That would be enough
That would be a start

THE BROKEN PATH TO CARE

The day my husband was taken from our home to the hospital was the day I began to learn about how challenging it is to get quality mental-health care. And the more I learned, the more devastating it was. It was traumatizing to witness my husband unravel before my eyes. It was equally traumatizing to figure out how to get help.

Getting help for Joe's mental-health issues was hard. It shouldn't have been, but it was. It's not as "easy" as when you feel physically sick and call for a medical appointment. Outside of hospitalization, the act of simply getting an appointment with a therapist took weeks, sometimes months (imagine if it took weeks to get an appointment to set a broken arm?). And seeing a therapist was just the first step in a long process that required vulnerability when Joe was feeling his least protected.

There is a lot about our mental-health system that is broken. And though it was absolutely worth all of the effort when Joe finally got the right help, it would be dishonest to leave out how hard it was to get good care. I'll describe some of what that looked like for us next.

What Care Costs Us

"But I don't understand. Where is all of our money going?"—this question asked of me with all sincerity by my then-very-ill husband.

I hung my head in frustration trying unsuccessfully once again to reconcile our monthly budget.

I don't remember answering. But I do remember running through the mental calculations in my head.

- Nonexistent work income: Due to blindness, his work hours had always been a bit inconsistent, but, since the day of his mental-health crisis the year prior, he hadn't worked at all, so there was the immediate loss of income
- High prescription costs: His medications changed frequently; he was generally on three at a time, and one of his medications had a $50 co-pay
- Co-pays for his bi-weekly weekly therapy
- Co-pays for his monthly psychiatry visits
- Co-pays for my weekly therapy
- Payments to ambulance companies for so kindly transporting him to the local psychiatric wards. How I made it to this point in adulthood having no idea that insurance didn't cover ambulance rides, I don't know—but they don't, or they didn't for us, anyway.

Where is all our money going? It was all I could do not to hold a mirror up to his confused face and scream *"To your care—it's all going to your care! How do you not understand that?"*

But I didn't pull out a mirror, and I didn't yell. I just felt defeat.

The loss of an income, coupled with the immediate added co-pay expense of $250 or so/month, not including surprise bills (e.g., ambulance rides), was a painful hit, but it took second place to the devastating day-to-day agony of simply living through a mental-health crisis. Money is just money, after all. But our people—the people we hold dear—are irreplaceable.

Financial Toll

I had always been the main breadwinner and kept our expenses pretty controlled. Then the financial expense of mental-health treatment hit. When Joe broke, things changed financially overnight. The expenses piled up quickly, and they weren't optional, not if I wanted my husband to live.

The burden of keeping our finances afloat was compounded by the stress of pouring money into his care and not knowing if any of it would work. It's not like other medical expenses, where, for example, we pay the co-pay, get prescribed a Z-Pac, and go home expecting relief within a few days. With these expenses, there was no quick fix, no guarantee, and no relief. It was like pouring all of our income into a high-risk investment, sitting back, crossing our fingers, and hoping that it would pay off.

Time Toll

In addition to the financial toll, the time—the sheer hours expended—to get treatment for mental-health issues cannot be ignored. From the time spent in emergency rooms awaiting assessment and intake, to the family meetings assessing progress at the hospital when he was inpatient, to the search for providers when he was released, and the staying in close contact with every provider either giving them information that they needed or receiving it, the volume of hours it took to coordinate and participate in care was daunting. I was fortunate to have a job that offered great benefits and generous time off. This allowed me to take days and weeks off and work odd hours so that I could spend time coordinating his care, make phone calls to insurance companies and providers, pore over expenses, organize rides, and schedule visits to reduce the time he would have to spend alone. This is a luxury many don't have.

During a particularly tough admission that first year, we had been at the ER for about six hours, waiting for a medical doctor to clear Joe so he could be admitted to a psychiatric unit. During those hours, Joe thought he might be God. Yep, that's still hard to write. It was harder to live. That is delusion, though. That is mania. That is psychosis. That is why we were at the hospital in the first place. During our wait, we had lots of time to talk, lucky me. He was sincerely confused about who he was and asked me what I thought. I told him that he wasn't God. He said, "If I'm not God, please make sure I never feel this way again." *I'm trying, buddy. I really am.* Joe was clearly in need of admission and just needed the medical doctor to do the formalities of signing off. I think that any provider with basic mental-health knowledge understands that it's not effective to argue with someone experiencing delusion. So I didn't love when this doctor finished up his physical exam with Joe, gave a snarky little laugh, and said: "Listen I'm a Christian. I believe in God, too. But that doesn't mean I think I'm God." I wish he could have just signed the papers and moved us along without feeling the need to add that little nugget. Congratulations on your spectacularly healthy brain, doc—may this never happen to you. I actually knew this doctor. He didn't remember me, but I had graduated from college with him 18 years prior. When I'm in a generous state of mind, I think he was probably a good doctor having a bad day. He had always seemed like a nice-enough person in college. But at this stage of life, I'm tired of being gracious in the face of bad behavior. Whatever kind of day that doctor was having, I was having a worse one. What do I really think of him? I think that doctor was a horse's ass.

Over that first year, Joe spent a total of almost two months in the hospital. Whatever hospital Joe was admitted to, I would call the nurses station every morning to check on his progress. I visited often. Despite the amount of time Joe spent admitted to inpatient care, there wasn't much opportunity to get to know his inpatient providers well. So the one time I found myself in an elevator alone with one of the nurses who was caring for Joe was memorable. We struck up a friendly conversation, and, when I told him who I was there to visit, he said, "I think Joe's going to be okay. What's happened to him isn't terribly unusual, and it just takes time. He is a really good guy." The elevator opened, and we parted ways—except now, I carried the impact of his kind comments with me. Now I carried within me the smallest glimpse of hope.

Emotional Toll

The emotional cost of mental illness is also worth mentioning. I was productive and effective in getting Joe the help he needed, but it came at a cost to me. It was beyond exhausting to live this way. I was depleted of both energy and joy. All of my energy was spent trying to help him. There was very little left of me to help me. The cruelty of being required—at the absolute darkest point in life—to advocate for your own care or a loved one's care cannot be properly put into words. So many times, I desperately wanted to stop and cry but didn't feel like I could. He always needed something, and it always felt urgent. When his therapy appointments didn't seem to be helping his progress, the urgency of finding him a new therapist consumed me. Any time spent in the care of an ineffective therapist was time wasted, time not getting well, or, in his case, time running out. Therapist or not, he was always close to giving up. I knew that, if he didn't get the care he needed, he would either end up back in the hospital, or, worse, he would end his life. The pattern of frantically changing therapists as we figured out they weren't working for him also played out with psychiatrists and day programs. Simply having assigned providers was not enough. We needed the right providers. Whether true or not, it felt like if I ever stopped trying to figure out his care, he might not make it. To have to carry within myself the weight of my incapacitated spouse's journey while simultaneously ensuring he was getting decent care, getting care for myself, holding together the finances, and attempting to be a reliable employee and otherwise decent human was almost too much to ask.

The associated costs of mental-health treatment in terms of dollars, time, and emotion add up quickly. Even if cost is not a factor, the infuriating truth is that a clear path to recovery doesn't exist. We are required to build the road we travel on to get the care we need. As someone who never built models or even the simplest of Lego creations as a child, you can imagine that the road I built wasn't exactly a paved masterpiece. It was more of a rutty path set precariously close to a cliff edge that we quite frequently fell right over. Somehow, the falls didn't end us, and we'd climb back up from each one and continue on the path. Joe's favorite saying every time we climbed back up after a fall was: "We are LeBlancs—we bounce; we don't splat." While that ended up being true, the path to recovery often felt like a hostile journey that some unknown powers had intentionally set up to be as confusing as possible. My problem was that I thought an effective mental-health system existed that would lead to healing as long as we did everything it required. I thought a path existed, but I just wasn't finding it. I'm glad I didn't know then that bushwhacking our way through the wilderness, building rudimentary paths along the way, was the only way anyone was getting care. An organized system of care beyond that didn't even exist.

The Battle for Good Care

We always encourage people who are struggling with mental-health issues to be brave and to reach out for help—and that is the right message. Yet the truth is that getting help is hard. I wish there were a Google Map to help us all navigate hospital admissions and insurance coverage. On a good day, it can be confusing to understand how insurance works and what it will cover. In times of crisis, it's near impossible to sort out.

Emergency Care

When my husband's first episode occurred, leading to his first emergency hospitalization, he was removed from our home by the police. That day, I didn't think twice about which hospital the ambulance would take him to or about the expertise or experience of the staff that might be assigned to his care. I didn't think we had a choice, and I didn't think to ask. His mind was delusional, and his behavior was threatening because he thought that the people coming to help him were really there to hurt him. He assaulted the police officers who came that day. I had never had reason to fear my husband, and now—watching as he was restrained and loaded into the ambulance—I was terrified at the thought of ever being in the same room with him again.

This is the reason why I went numb a few hours later when the hospital called to tell me he was ready to be picked up to come home. I listened quietly as the nurse relayed these words to me over the phone, but I remember not feeling the terror that would have been appropriate. Instead, discouragement was the feeling that my body let rise to the top. It would be more than a year later before I could begin to acknowledge or process the terror I felt during this time, from the initial incident and throughout the coming chaotic months. But in that moment on the phone with the discharge nurse, I needed to function, and discouragement was the emotion that would allow me to do so.

My heart sank. Did they not know what we had just been through? They wouldn't release someone who was still dangerous, would they? Maybe he got better? Soon after, Joe called me directly to confirm that he could come home. But his voice was not his. His tone was all wrong. I didn't think I had a choice, so I gathered up my courage and drove to the hospital to pick him up. That the hospital had decided to release him without talking to me or to the police about the events that got him there in the first place only solidified the unspoken message: I should not expect support—even from the places whose job it was to help him.

Fortunately—and I realize this might be a strange choice of words—my presence at the hospital that morning sent him back into psychosis in such a grand way that he earned himself admittance. My husband had not been properly assessed for safety, so I left that visit with bruises on me. My bruises—the additional trauma to me—are what got him admitted that day. It was a high price to pay for admission.

There are many steps involved in accessing care through our mental-health system and assessing someone for safety (e.g., threat to self or others) is pretty much step one. For reasons that I will never know but that probably had to do with the hospital staff's lack of training and experience, this particular hospital failed miserably at step one. This experience was my earliest indicator that our mental-health system is broken at the hospital-admission level.

When I think back on this day now, from a safe, healed distance, I am angry at this chain of events. What gaping holes in our law-enforcement and hospital systems created an environment where I was asked to bring home a psychotic husband less than five hours after he'd been pulled from our home and assaulted police? What a supremely craptastic position for me to have been put into. What a useless system.

I don't know if this was another case of me suppressing feelings or not, but I don't recall being angry at Joe that day. I was afraid of him but not angry. And I was sad because I knew that our marriage was over if this new version of him wasn't fixable. His actions had terrified me, yet somewhere deep inside, I knew that the person before me wasn't really him. Which is very confusing because . . . it was him. But he did this when his mind was broken in a place that was supposed to protect him and also in a place that was supposed to protect me. After what had occurred at our house that morning, what happened in the ER never should have taken place.

Inpatient Care

I had no idea how insurance worked but soon learned that, upon inpatient admission, insurance would cover just three days of care and then re-evaluate his condition every few days thereafter until discharge. Though it's hard to live like this—worried sick about your loved one but also not being able to plan more than three days ahead—I was happy that he was safe. My first bump up against insurance companies came when the hospital started speaking about releasing him, though his delusions had not lifted, and I had not been alone in a room with him since he was pulled from our home. I was asked to come to a care-plan meeting at the hospital to discuss next steps. My Mom and a kind friend from church accompanied me to this meeting. It was the first time I had seen Joe since the ER. We gathered around a very large conference table and I intentionally sat at the opposite end from him because I was still scared. After a few minutes, I felt comfortable enough to sit next to him and talk for a few minutes. He wasn't scary anymore, but he was not well. He was still talking in circles thinking he was making sense.

Next, the doctor asked that we meet without Joe in another room. At this meeting, they informed me that Joe was going to be discharged in the next few days. When I asked in all honesty where he was going to be discharged to (because after what I'd already been through, they wouldn't expect me to take him back into our home when he was still fully delusional, would they?), the doctor simply said, "That's not my problem." I can still feel these words in my bones clear as day. I do remember feeling fear that day. I also remember hating the doctor that day. I think the problem with mental illness is exactly this . . . no one really knows what to do about it. No one owns it. It is no one's problem. And spouses like me are the no ones whose problem it becomes. Looking back now, I realize that our insurance had stopped paying for care, so the doctor didn't have much of a choice. Still, this doctor could have benefited from a refresher course in compassion. She offered me none of that.

Later that day, I spent hours on the phone with our insurance company pleading with the behavioral-health representative to keep him in the hospital until he was more well. She assured me that they would pay for him to be there until he was safe.

She lied.

They released Joe in full delusion the day before Thanksgiving. When I refused to pick him up because I was still scared of him, Joe's sister graciously opened her home to him. He was instructed to begin a day program the day after Thanksgiving at a hospital closer to us. To say that his behavior at his sister's home was concerning during those forty-eight hours after he was released would be an understatement. I will always be thankful to her for taking him in when the hospital put him out. When he showed up for his day program at the new hospital two days later—still incredibly disoriented and confused—staff immediately admitted him, even before getting approval from insurance. The new hospital's staff said they could not, in good conscience, release him into the community, so they kept him, and this is where I first saw what it looked like to have a strong, compassionate, curious team gather around someone suffering a mental-health crisis and walk him toward hope. This team cared about Joe. When I called each day to ask how he was, they gave me medical updates but also took the time to give examples of funny things he had said. I felt the relief that can only come from knowing your loved one is in good hands. We learned during this second hospitalization that the medicines he had been prescribed during the first hospitalization had become toxic to him and were exacerbating his delusions. His brain cleared dramatically when the medicines were adjusted. The insurance company eventually agreed to cover the costs for this second hospitalization, but I will never forget that they took him before approval came through.

Joe remembers very little of that first hospitalization. When I tell him he was in the first hospital for almost a month, he can't believe it. He remembers two weeks of it. He was so heavily drugged. I, however, remember every delusional phone conversation with him. Sometimes I wish it were the opposite. I wish I didn't remember conversations with him when his brain was that broken.

I wish I could say that once he was discharged from the second hospital, he got better and never struggled again. But that would not be true. Months later, Joe would find himself back in that very hospital when his mental health plummeted yet again. From the start, though, I knew he was in good hands. His care team took into account that Joe was blind and cared enough to research and confirm a condition that occurs during end-stage blindness called Charles Bonnet syndrome. This temporary syndrome causes people to see things—specifically children with crooked teeth and textures on walls—that are not there. Joe absolutely experienced both of these hallucinations right there in the waiting room. As we were waiting to get him admitted to the very hospital that would diagnosis this for him, he turned to me and said, "Did a little kid with messed-up teeth just walk through that doctor's legs?" During that same wait, he got up to feel the walls because he thought something was hanging on them. I sank deeper into myself with every comment he made because the reality he was describing was not mine. I thought, *How can he be sitting here, months into this awful season of our lives, getting sicker by the minute?* Joe was once again given excellent care by this hospital. He was treated effectively and shown great kindness. They let me bring him his favorite takeout sandwiches several times each week. His providers kept me in the loop, sought my input, and listened when I provided it. They made me feel like we were all on "Team Joe." He improved so much under their care.

Despite a mental-health system broken at the hospital-admission level, the experience with this new hospital reminded us that there also exists—at least in small pockets—groups of dedicated staff who know how to work around the broken parts of the system to help put people in crisis back together.

Outpatient Care

When Joe was released from the hospital with instructions to attend therapy, figuring out which providers would take our insurance was only the beginning. The bigger question for me was always, are the people who take our insurance going to be able to help him? Would the providers we went to really be able to provide?

During this time, he was covered by the private insurance I carried through work, and he also had Medicare as a payer of last resort due to blindness. By the time he was ready to leave the hospital, his delusions were clearing, and his biggest issue was a deepening depression. As a requirement of discharge, the hospital set him up with both a provider and prescriber appointment in the community. But we learned pretty quickly that sometimes assigned providers are not the most competent. They are just the most available, and there very well might be a reason that they have so many open appointments.

The First Prescriber

The first outpatient prescriber that my husband was assigned to by the hospital discharge team put him on Prozac, which—if it is to be effective—takes about eight weeks to begin working. Eight weeks is a lot of time to ask of someone who wants to die every hour on the hour. But we gave it the old college try. It didn't feel like we had a choice. Eight miserable weeks later, with not a bit of relief in sight, we asked the prescriber to consider another medication. He begrudgingly agreed to switch. Within days, the new medication caused my husband's hands and arms to shake uncontrollably. Joe had read about tardive dyskinesia and was terrified thinking that the shaking was never going to stop. We called the prescriber several times that week. He was slow to return calls. We felt stuck: scared to stop the medicine, and scared to continue it. When we finally made contact, this prescriber opted to put my husband back on Prozac, quality of life be damned. When we asked if there was any other medication we could try, we were told simply "No." Note—don't ever tell a traumatized, sleep-deprived wife fighting for her husband's life and armed with Google that we are out of options after trying only two medications. Just don't. I began making plans to find another prescriber.

The First Therapist

In the meantime, the therapist that Joe had been assigned to at that same practice didn't seem to be resonating. A few weeks later, I invited myself to sit in on a session and listened as the provider shared that he himself had been diagnosed with bipolar but that he didn't need medication. His voice escalated many times into a yell during the sessions. In my opinion, he absolutely needed medication, a nap, and possibly Jesus as well—I don't really know. I had a lot of problems to solve. He wasn't going to be one of them. It was time to leave that practice.

While our hospital experiences had made it clear that the mental-health system at the hospital level was broken, this provider and prescriber experience made it clear that the mental-health system at the provider level—including oversight of the methods used by providers and prescribers—was also broken. The systems set up to help us weren't doing a very good job. The search for a strong therapist/prescriber team began.

Changing Providers

We changed therapists and prescribers several times that year. We changed because some—like those mentioned above—seemed incompetent. Others along the way weren't as bad, but they seemed to lack true concern for who my husband was before the break and for the person he could become. They didn't seem invested in his care, so the care they provided was sloppy and generic. In my opinion, they had written him off. They didn't have any expectations for his recovery, and I guess I still did.

I started the search by pulling up lists of providers from our insurance company's website and cross-referencing the names with word-of-mouth referrals from friends, neighbors, co-workers, and basically anyone at all who said they knew of mental-health providers who had been effective. An added difficulty was that—due to blindness—my husband does not drive, so we could consider only those providers that he would be able to get to using public transportation or that I would be able to drive him to after work (or, in some cases, during work, which is how things played out that first year). We also thought that it would make sense logistically to find a provider and prescriber who worked for the same practice. I took detailed notes as I worked my way through pages of recommended therapists and prescribers, calling them to explain my husband's current state of mind and asking about their experience and/or interest in treating someone like my husband. If their wait lists were full, my next question would always be "Who would you recommend I call next?" It took research into more than twelve providers (I stopped counting after that) and more than a year to find people who were competent. Finding providers with an open slot within the next month or so that also took our insurance and who had some level of interest in taking on the complicated case I described to them (blind, previously delusional, actively suicidal) was not easy.

A Strong Provider Team

Three prescribers, six medication regimens, three therapists, four hospitalizations, and almost one year later, we finally found a therapist and provider team that worked.

The therapist we settled on treated my husband like the human being he was, and insurance covered all but the co-pay for these visits. After a while, this therapist—in an act of true compassion—would secretly give me back the co-pays that Joe brought into the appointments each week. He truly wanted to help us. This speaks again to the pockets of kindness that exist along this journey.

The prescriber we found was just as amazing, but the road to him included some added drama. While he did not work in the same practice as the therapist, he was approachable, down to earth, and curious. We liked that in a provider. Joe was still actively depressed, but he could sense that this prescriber cared about him as a person. We connected with this prescriber strongly at our first meeting, only to learn at the end of the session that he could not take our insurance. More specifically, though we had private insurance, which he normally would take, by contract he was not allowed to take insurance payment from anyone who also had Medicare. When he explained this to us at the end of our first meeting, I left defeated. I sat in the car in the parking lot and wept for an hour. My husband just sat beside me in silence, not able to process feelings at that time. I felt like we had finally found someone who could help, and, now, we were not going to have access to him. It almost broke me.

A week later, I called this prescriber back and asked if it was allowable to pay out of pocket and, if so, what the actual rates would be. It was $250 for the initial consult and $75 per session. We decided to make it work and pay out of pocket. At first, seeing him a few times each month was hard and expensive. Later, Joe was well enough to go every three months, and that was more doable. Most importantly, this psychiatrist was thoughtful in the way he worked with Joe to make treatment decisions, and, as a result, the treatment was successful. The decision to pay out of pocket was one of the best decisions of our lives. And I accept it for the privilege that it is, knowing that this option is not available to many others who don't have the extra income needed for out-of-pocket payments.

It's All Connected

The scary truth is this:

- The hospitals that we are admitted to will keep us only as long as the insurance that we have pays them to.
- The providers that we see are limited to those covered by the insurance that we have.
- The quality and style of the therapy that we receive are determined by the individual therapist we are seeing.
- The medications that we are prescribed—and the order in which they are offered—are determined by the professional preferences of the prescribers that we see.

It's all connected. And our survival depends on all of it.

Insurance companies are the gatekeepers of our access to providers, and we can only hope that the needs of patients are primary as decisions are made about who can see which providers, for how long, and at what cost.

Prescribers are the gatekeepers of our medication options, and we can only hope that they are driven by their own passion for the field and their ability to see each patient as unique and worthy of relief.

In addition to the trauma of the actual mental-health issue or event that drives a person to need care in the first place, it is my experience that the process of navigating the costs of care, making sense of the rules that hospitals and insurance companies must follow, and finding effective therapists and prescribers can be a secondary trauma unto itself.

Our mental-health system is badly broken in many places, and I don't believe that we would tolerate a medical system this broken. We wouldn't allow doctors to refuse admission if our loved ones showed up needing emergency surgery, and we would file a complaint if a doctor tried to send us home without stitching up an open wound. The ongoing challenge is that medical treatments are more concrete (e.g., set a broken arm, stitch an open wound) while mental-health treatments are still a work in progress. We are all still learning how best to treat mental-health issues, and, so, there are lots of mistakes made along the way.

I hope someday that those who go through what we've survived have it a bit easier. I hope loved ones don't have to lose sleep over the costs of care or have to question the compassion of their insurance company or the competency of a provider. I hope no one else has to feel defeated trying answer the question, "Where is all of our money going?" while doing the best they can.

I close my eyes sometimes and think of how things could have been if my husband had been brought immediately after that first psychiatric event into a hospital that understood what he needed, surrounded him with care, kept him until he was well, and then handed him off thoughtfully to a provider/prescriber team hand-picked with his success in mind. This was not to be our experience—but someday, if we keep talking about it and keep working on our broken selves and our broken systems until they are whole—maybe there will eventually be a well-traveled path to care that those who come after us can easily find.

Until then, the best we can do
is keep helping each other along;
walking each other toward healing
on this broken path to care.

A SHOUT OUT TO EMDR

I think because the universe knew I couldn't take much more, I hit the jackpot with my own therapist. She was the perfect companion to walk me through the darkest time of my life.

I didn't cry at all during weekly talk therapy that first year. I was too stunned, consumed with all that had to be done to figure out how to help my husband survive. I was in pain, for sure, but my focus was on doing whatever could be done to get Joe better—I thought that when his pain stopped, mine would, too. My weekly therapy sessions grounded me, provided a safe place for me to talk openly about the ugliest realities of my new life, and helped me figure out what actions I could take the next week to get through it. There was no predictability, nothing consistent about our life. I remember not being able to think or plan more than a couple of days ahead.

It took a year to establish a rhythm with Joe's care and to settle into a routine of appointments with a therapist and psychiatrist that seemed to want the best for Joe. I wouldn't go so far as to say Joe was getting better after a year, but he was not getting worse. At that point, I wasn't sure if he would find his way again. I wasn't sure if the version of Joe that existed at that time was as good as it was going to get, given all he had endured.

After a year of very helpful weekly talk therapy for me, some of the more difficult memories that I was carrying as a result of the initial trauma were becoming unmanageable. Most notably, I began crying whenever I saw an ambulance, passed a hospital, or encountered any vehicle with a siren blaring. This reaction was frustrating and not within my control. A delayed shock reaction . . . the result of the worst of the memories feeling safe enough to surface and ask to be dealt with. I am nothing if not logical, but these reactions were separate from logic. At this point, my therapist encouraged me to try EMDR (Eye Movement Desensitization and Reprocessing), a form of therapy that helps process traumatic memories and put them at a safe distance so they are more manageable.

Trust me when I say that the last thing that I wanted to do was explain the events of that past year to a brand-new specialty therapist, but the thought of randomly bursting into tears for the rest of my days was even less appealing. The good news is that EMDR can be a task-specific endeavor. I went into it knowing it was specifically to help me deal with my memories and that, once those were addressed, I could go back to my original therapist and continue regular talk therapy.

I knew EMDR would be intense but had underestimated how much so. With EMDR you talk a little at first, high level about one or two of the hardest memories and then—it's hard to explain, but, with the therapist in the room and the help of some devices that alternately buzz held in each hand, you close your eyes and let your mind wander to the worst memory and then go wherever it goes from there. Every few minutes, the therapist will stop the process and ask, *What are you thinking about now?* You respond with a sentence or two and then close your eyes and return to letting your mind wander from the memory you just mentioned to wherever else your mind wants to go. There are no wrong answers, no wrong memories. Sometimes when the therapist asked what memory I was thinking about, it wasn't a painful one at all. Mostly, though, my mind went to places my heart had refused to go up until then. My job was just to tell her and keep letting my mind go where it needed to go.

I sobbed my way through every session. It wasn't an option, and no one was more surprised than me. Crying in front of strangers is not my thing. At times during our sessions, when asking what memory I was thinking of, she would make me stop for a minute to take a drink of water. Maybe to replace the water pouring out of my eyes, I'm not sure. I remember her easing my embarrassment by saying that she had a few clients who were construction workers that come in on their lunch hour, and even they sob their way through sessions. It's part of the process. It taps into the deepest, most unspeakable pain and lets your brain look at it again and feel what has been pushed down deep.

Due to the intensity of the sessions, the EMDR therapist I went to was adamant that each session needed to take two hours. Though my insurance at that time would only cover forty-five-minute sessions, this kindhearted soul spent two full hours per session with me, rather than abbreviate our time or ask me to pay extra. I will never forget her generosity. This treatment was life changing to me.

EMDR saved me. After four sessions, the weight of inner pain that I was carrying lifted. The memories still hurt me deeply, but it was almost as if they were put behind glass. I could see them, but they could not touch me. I do not understand how it all works, but I do know that, after that, I could drive by hospitals, ambulances, and police cars without crying.

Forever

I am forever never the same
Forever altered

But not
Forever lacking joy
Forever dead inside
Forever disconnected from life
Forever apathetic about the future
Forever disappointed
Forever distraught
Forever damaged
Forever angry
Forever tearful
Forever broken
Forever afraid
Forever humiliated
Forever done trying
Forever wishing this was not my life
Forever hating every minute of this

I am forever never the same
Forever altered

But it won't stay this way forever

At least that's what I'm told

ONE MONTH

One of the hardest parts of living through this time in my life was realizing that those around me had no idea how hard my life was every single day, even years later. It made complete sense that they had no idea because I didn't talk about it. There was no spare energy for that. Everything I had went into preserving his survival as well as my own. The days were brutal, and I didn't have words to explain why. One month, I decided to write down on paper what exactly was making life so hard. It is a pretty horrible read, but it was not an unusual month. Here is a glimpse of what families living with those with acute mental illness might be living. Our stories will differ, but I believe the depth of pain is similar.

Exhale

I sit at my desk at work listening for sirens going in the direction of the train station. He gets out of school right around now. It will take him about three minutes to get to the station and a few more minutes for the train to come. Will this be the day? Time passes. Then more time. No sirens. I exhale now. He has not ended his life today, at least not by jumping in front of the train intended to pick him up and bring him home. He hasn't said that this is his intention. He is way too smart for that. Words like that get him a stay in the hospital, and, after four stays already, he is not going back. Ever. But his whole person oozes suicide. He has disengaged from life. He lives on the fringe of conversations. It's trickier this time, because he doesn't show the typical signs of depression or at least the signs that he had before. He is not sleeping all day. He is up and showered. He goes to school. His appetite is fine. But he is distant. He is here but not here. He has given up. And when I ask him about it, he doesn't deny it. But he doesn't say the words that get him hospitalized. I don't blame him. I wouldn't, either. His last few years have been nothing short of hell. His future isn't looking so good, either. When is enough, enough? I don't know. If I were looking ahead at a difficult life, knowing that I didn't have the strength to do what needed to be done to make it better, I might consider that enough, too. Either way, it's not my decision to make.

I pull into my driveway at day's end and sit there in the dark, taking deep breaths, steeling myself for what might await me when I walk in the door. Will he be hanging? If he is, what will I do? I already know. I will take him down. I will sit with him quietly for a while—an hour maybe—before I call anyone. Then I will invite the world in.

I walk into the house, and he is there. Alive. I exhale. He has not ended his life today by hanging. We talk about this. I say, "I will be so angry if, after all I've been through (yes, all *I've* been through) the past few years, if I am the one to come home and find you dead. If I have to process these memories along with all the others . . . " Later, he tells me he had specific plans to hang himself in our home. I knew that. Without words being exchanged, I knew what he was planning. What stopped him was that he couldn't figure out how to do this and not have me be the one to find him. One solution he came up with was to call 911, put the phone down and hang himself immediately. But we live . . . two minutes . . . from the police station. And what if they got to him before he was dead? He couldn't solve that. And he didn't want me to find him. So he didn't do it.

Drugged

More days go by. I come home from work. We walk the dog. We start making pizza for dinner. Joe mentions that his head hurts. His vision is wavy and blurry. He tries to spread sauce on the pizza and makes a huge mess. Bigger than usual. I tell him it's okay and to go sit down while I make dinner. We talk about how this could be his eyes changing again, and that, hopefully, his headache will go away and the waviness will subside. I read him an article I found on end-stage Retinitis Pigmentosa that talks about dizziness being common. We eat. He is distant. Quiet. I tell him to lie down on the couch. I go to Zumba. It's only for an hour, and I need it. I come home to confusion. He is nearly comatose. Sitting upright. Speaking jumbled words. Delusional. I am devastated. He hasn't been delusional for years. I can't imagine how this could have come on so quickly without more signs. I sit. I think. I ask him, "Do we need to go to the hospital?" "No," he says. I am sick inside. I do not know what to do. If he is delusional, he needs the hospital. I ask him to tell me about his day. I am looking for clues as to what has gone wrong. After a long hour of convoluted back-and-forth conversation, he admits that he took some pills. I look at him, furious. But I must be calm because he is not really there, and I don't want to waste my rage on someone who can't grasp it. I had already purged the house of almost every old prescription medication. I had kept only three bottles. Hidden them well. Bottles with heavy-hitting pills. Pills I hadn't needed in months but kept in order to help me sleep if the awful insomnia I had early on returned. Pills that were painkillers from an old surgery that had never been taken but were kept just in case. That day, he had searched through the house looking for pills to take. Any pills. And he found them. He found them. How many did you take? Just a couple. Which ones did you take? I don't know. I am furious but I must be calm and smart. He has drugged himself. Was this a suicide attempt? Even if it wasn't, did he take enough pills to kill him? How will the pills he took interact with the prescription medicine he is legitimately supposed to take? Should I take him to get his stomach pumped? *I don't know.* How am I supposed to know? I am done. I decide he is okay enough to sleep it off. Deep inside, I decide that, if this kills him, this is what he wanted anyway. He is alive but dead right now. Being dead, dead is almost more honest.

He is making no sense. He is a mess. Before I put him to bed, I record him with my phone because I will be damned if I am living through another delusional night with Joe with no witnesses. I will make him watch this when he is clearheaded. I don't care if he can't see. I will make him listen to himself. And hear what he has put me through. I lift him up. He is deadweight. He has to lean fully on me to take the tiniest of steps. I walk him to the bathroom. He has to pee but can't hold his man part. So I hold it for him because it means one less mess for me to clean up. Next, I put him to bed. He sits on the bed motionless. I lift each limb up onto the bed because he can't function enough to move. I tell him to lie down, and he doesn't know how; so I push his chest down. It is reminiscent of his early days after his original unraveling. He is helpless. His brain is gone.

I sleep on the couch. I am furious. He gets up at 2 a.m. to pee. He comes into the living room and says, "I slept in my clothes?" He is honestly confused. I tell him to go to bed. In the morning, as I leave for work, he says "What happened last night?" I am furious. I am done. I go to work. Later he emails an apology. He is remorseful. I am done. I am so tired of this life.

This was one month in my life.

This particular month happened four years—48 months—after my husband's original breakdown. There were 47 additional fun-filled months prior to this one about which I could share the details as well, but it's really hard finding an audience for content like this.

So when I say my life has changed, I mean my life has changed.

When I say his original break wasn't a long-ago terrible day that is over and done but rather the starting point of an incredibly difficult and painful life, this is what I mean.

When I say my beliefs have had to be reconciled to the life before me, this is the life I mean.

When I say I don't have time for people who look at me in ways that say, I should be better, believe stronger, and be more recovered by this point, this is why.

It would be so much better if people would just simply believe me when I say

Everything has changed.

On a side note:

I will talk more in later pages about the impact of the religious beliefs I had at the time and how they had to change. But right now I will say this:

What a terrible burden it was to live through these years believing that God could have stopped this at any time but chose not to.

What a terrible feeling it was to think that these hellish times were intentionally "allowed" for my good and planned for my life. That misguided belief alone prolonged my pain more than I will ever be able to articulate.

I wasted so much time begging God for mercy, begging God to make this end.

All of the energy I exerted begging God for relief was energy that I did not have—wasted energy that robbed me of any peace I might otherwise have had.

I understand now that God does not work like that. God does not send relief down from the skies. God does not bring or stop or end the tragedies in this world. I believe now that God sees it all but is outside of it all, and that any relief God sends is done by sending people to come alongside through the pain.

I grieve for how much easier it would have been had I not brought my misguided beliefs to this horrible time. It would have just been a terrible thing that happened to us. Not an intentional life wrecking. It still would have been terrible, but it would not have been personal.

Blood Runs Cold

First
Your blood
Runs cold

Then
You make
Your feet move

And you do
And you solve
And you comfort

And you get
The people
You love
The help
They need

Only later
Do you
Feel

And when you do
The feelings
Take you
To the ground

Where you stay
Until you
Remember
How to breathe

And when you are ready
You inhale
And rise up

And steady yourself
For whatever
Your mentally ill loved one
Needs next

ABOUT FRIENDSHIPS

On that very first awful day, I was surrounded with love and support. The amazing friend from church whom I called first when I ran out of the house that day at 5:30 in the morning, showed up within minutes. The day before, Joe had been saying he wanted to meet with this particular friend to talk about the "insights" he was having about the Bible. I know now that those insights were mania, but I didn't know that at the time. This friend is a lawyer, and my initial words to him on the phone that morning were: "Something is wrong with Joe. He is in the house screaming, but I don't want him to get arrested. What should I do?" This friend wisely advised me to get the police, so I did.

My parents lived an hour away and didn't flinch when they got my early-morning call saying, "Something is wrong with Joe. The police are here. Please come." Together, we sat around the kitchen table, trying to make sense of what was happening. Not long after, friends from church showed up with bagels and comforting words.

Then my childhood friend appeared out of nowhere with potted plants for every room of my home.

She instinctively knew that something important had died.

She knew that I'd need to see reminders all around me to prove life after this point was possible.

In those blurry early days that followed, family and friends from my neighborhood, church, work, and gym checked in on me often and cared for me well. They came to the hospital with me. They visited Joe on their own. They listened as I told them what doctors were saying about Joe's next steps. They texted me kind words. They invited me places and allowed me to show up sad.

As months went by, Joe didn't get much better. At times, he got worse. We had wonderful friends, but the days of carefree, easy friendship were over. Friends who knew only the version of Joe that was funny, happy, and positive did not know what to think of the version of Joe that was silent, stone-faced, and angry. I could see it sometimes—the struggle of friends who didn't know what to do. Who cared about Joe but didn't want to come over more than once, because, when they did, Joe sat in silence and didn't engage. I could see some friends looking impatiently at Joe, wondering when he was going to be back to his old self so life could resume as normal. I didn't have words then to help them understand that Joe was going to be unrecognizable for a very long time. I was just barely grasping that concept myself. He looked fine physically, but his insides were the emotional equivalent of someone who had narrowly survived a car wreck and was being held together with a full body cast. Though it would be crazy to expect a physically wrecked friend to return friendship from within a body cast, some seemed to expect this from mentally wrecked Joe. They wanted the old version of Joe back, and that version was not available. I would guess that sitting silently beside someone in a body cast is probably easier than sitting silently beside someone with a broken mind. Mental illness has a way of making family and friends feel helpless. And when people feel helpless, sometimes they leave.

Joe wasn't the only one who had changed. Friends who were used to me having a peaceful, contented demeanor didn't know what to do with the version of me that was anxious and distracted. Sadness was the biggest part of me. I wasn't the same. Many desperately wanted the old me to return. But old me no longer existed. I couldn't go out and have fun with people because I could barely go out at all. Fun wasn't appealing. Rest was. I couldn't enter into other people's lives in any meaningful way because I was drowning in the life I was living with Joe.

So we lost people.

Life before mental illness felt like being on a full bustling train alongside everyone in our lives. Life was rich and full in the way it is when you have shared common experiences. But as the train rolled down the tracks of Joe's illness, each time it stopped, people hopped off. Some got off at the very first stop. Others made it much later down the line. Mental illness is hard to be around. Most people who have a choice get off the train. It made me sad then, but I get it now. I've done the same thing to people in my own life. I've looked at devastating circumstances that those around me were going through and decided how involved I wanted to be, based on how close I was with that person. That's the luxury we have when it's not happening directly to us. We can't ride the train with everyone in pain, or we'd never have time to live. We have to be strategic with our energy.

Though our train seemed way too empty years into this life we didn't choose, I'm happy to report that those who opted to stay on the train with us for the duration of the trip were all we needed.

There were exquisitely beautiful things that happened years deep into our journey. There were people who drove Joe to therapy appointments every week smack dab in the middle of the day so I wouldn't have to take time off of work. There was the friend who invited us to parties, always with the reminder to just come as we were, no happiness required. What a gift to be able to show up and not be judged for being in pain. There was the friend who took Joe to spinning classes, bought a tandem bike, outfitted Joe with all the required bike gear, and became a consistent riding partner. Joe still carried sadness within him, but these rides reconnected him with his love of the outdoors and his love of riding. They reminded him what friendship felt like. They reminded him that he was worthy of good things in life and that he could still be happy.

So many friends were beautiful to me, too. But I didn't feel like myself for years. I remember showing up at a friend's birthday party, happy for the change of scenery but dazed and no longer clear how to exist normally in the world anymore. Other friends invited me out for long walks in the woods and let me talk freely about how hard life still was. Or out for coffee, where I could be honest about the state of my life over latte. Few people have the patience to really listen to another person's pain, but these friends showered me with grace and let me say my ugly truths. When they didn't collapse under the details of my story or the weight of my words, I knew that I wouldn't collapse, either.

Who I Was Before

I'm not
Who I was
Before

That person
Was swept away
With my old life

So when people act
Like nothing has changed
Either because
They don't know it has
Or because
They don't want to admit it has

It is confusing

Nice but
Kind of offensive

Like getting
A compliment
On something
You no longer
Own

A little painful
Disappointing people
With who I am

A little painful
All the love

For the me
I used to be

Not much
For the me
I am now

DEEP GRIEF

There is a hellish level of ongoing grief that no amount of money can relieve. An alternate world where one may function but truly be living on the fringe. For me, grief showed itself in several different ways:

The Inability to Listen to Music

I had always loved music but during these years, I needed silence. Every sound was jarring to me. Even the car radio was off limits, its sound too much for me to take in. Just another thing for me to process when my internal processor was already maxed.

Half Listening

For years, I found it almost impossible to stay firmly rooted in normal life while managing the chaos of my personal life. Oh, I may have *looked* like I was taking in the normalcy around me, but I wasn't. I had no capacity left. I remember a rare day at work when I did have spare mental space to actually ask questions about how the lives of those around me were going. That day I came within seconds of almost asking a co-worker how her wedding plans were coming along. I caught myself just in time. She had been married for three months by that point. This is one of a few embarrassing near misses. Another was when a co-worker began telling me about a friend of a friend who had passed away, and I immediately told her that I was so sorry to hear that. She looked at me with confusion and said, "But I told you last week that this person had passed away." I had no memory of that earlier conversation. Information was coming at me, but I was not retaining. I used to be good at carrying other people's pain but I had changed into someone who could barely handle her own. I was only half-listening to the conversations around me because I was only half-existing.

Many times, I was annoyed with Joe because he showed no interest in anything outside of his sad, sick world. He took all of my mental energy. 100% of it. He took it as if it was owed to him. He took it as if to say "See—I *told* you that no amount of effort will bring me back to life." Joe was so distracted by his own pain that other people didn't exist in his world, not even me. Ironic isn't it, that I was doing the same thing? I was so filled up with what was going on in my home life that what was going on in the lives of the people around me barely registered. None of this disconnect was intentional. It was just a casualty of life with mental illness.

The Missing of Normal Interactions

I was in a constant state of vigilance, daily trying to find the magic program, therapist, or activity that would move Joe forward. Dear friends tried their best to help get me out of my brain. They would invite me to venture out to the mall for dinner and shopping which had always been fun for us in the past. The past was gone, though, and I could barely make it through dinner before the pain of my reality and how different it was from those around me would rise up and require me to leave as soon as the check was paid. I would make it to my car and cry all the way home. It was simply too painful to be around people whose worlds were not actively burning down.

The Missing of Normal-Sized Problems

I remember listening to someone in my life struggling with the choice of which wood-floor style to go with and feeling the bittersweet pain of wishing that flooring choice was my most pressing issue.

There was also:

- The constant internal agony of wondering where I was on this journey, when it would end, and what I would do if it didn't.
- The painful question of "Does this really happen to people—or only to people like me?"
- The realization that this will always be a part of my life story and the wondering if the rest of the story is worth being around for.

I never knew a pain could go so deep.

Beyond

There is a
Black and lonely
Place of grief
That exists
Beyond tears
Beyond the comfort of God's words
Possibly beyond the reach of God
Definitely beyond the reach of people
Though they sacrifice much to comfort

Frighteningly beyond
Unexplainably beyond

And if you are there
The best you can do
Is hope beyond hope
To get back to
The place of tears
The place where God can comfort
The place where people can comfort
The place where there is air
To help you breathe
Through the pain

Still a difficult
Place of grief
To be sure
But not as difficult
As the place beyond

Grief

When grief
First arrives
It greets you
With a slap in the face
Drags you around
By your broken heart
Takes you where it will
Has no regard for your comfort
No respect for your peace of mind

Later on
When you are a little
Better acquainted
You drag grief around
Make a place for it
In your broken heart
Take it where you will
Introduce it to comfort
Make it befriend peace

And though grief
Lacks the most basic of manners
You are much nicer to grief
Than it ever was to you
Giving it a pillow to rest on
When it tires
Letting it breathe
And expand
Or hibernate

Whatever it needs
You give it
Because it is a part of you
But it is not all of you

When grief
First arrives
It takes over
And you feel
Only pain
Every minute
No relief

Later on
You start to feel
Something
Other than grief
Stirring inside
Filling in around the pain
It is familiar but mysterious
And you can't quite place it

And then you do recognize it
And place it
And invite it
To come alongside grief
And teach grief manners
And show grief its place

It is Strength

A trusted old friend
Returned
After a long time gone

SOMETIMES THINGS FALL APART

We don't get to pick the devastation that comes into our lives. Sometimes things just fall apart. No one consults with us first about the type or cadence of the catastrophes that are coming our way. No one asks our preferred type of tragedy or inquires as to whether now might be a good time for it to arrive. Crisis is a bit rude that way. It won't be ignored. It must be acknowledged. When it comes in, it knocks us to the ground for a good while, always longer than we'd like. The pain levels us.

Blindness and mental illness are apparently the assigned catastrophes in my life thus far. I don't know that I would have chosen them, but here they are.

Whatever life brings us, at some point, we get up. We survey our surroundings, nod toward the wreckage, and keep walking. We have to walk because running doesn't work. As much as we want to be able to race through life's terrible seasons, the crushing realization is that some pains cannot be outrun. We have to walk with pain within us and beside us for a very long time, until one day, we find peace again.

Outrun

I get
So tired
Of trying
To outrun
Pain

Pain
That has already
Taken
Too much

Pain
That I would like
Some distance
From

Pain
That I can feel
Coming closer
Again

Pain
That wants only
To take from me

And I don't want
To give it
Any more

And that is why

Though I'm so
Very tired
Of running

I run

Sometimes Things Fall Apart

Sometimes
Things fall
Apart

Completely
Unexpectedly
Unfathomably

Everything
That matters
Destroyed

And all
That can
Be done

Is nothing, really

Only wait
Bear witness
Give name
To the pain
That took
Everything

Maybe one day
Years later
Relearn
To breathe

Maybe one day
Write the story
Of what you've
Lived through

Maybe one day
Look the ending
Loss has written you
Dead in the eyes

Hold its gaze

Pick up a pen
Rewrite

MOMENTS OF STRENGTH

Trying to live any kind of normal life during the chaos of Joe's mental-health issues was a battle. There were moments, though, in spite of the nightmare, when I felt strong.

Here is one. Despite being exhausted for four solid years as I navigated my suffocating little life, I still managed to return 100% of my library books on time. Nothing screams, "I am still a functioning member of this society" while your world is burning down like ensuring that books are returned in a timely manner out of respect for the next reader. It might not seem like much, but I distinctly remember being so freaking proud of myself for that one. The bar for my happiness was clearly set pretty low.

I also felt strong during Zumba class, which I faithfully attended at least three times a week. During class, I got to spend lighthearted time with friends. I got to be around happy, hopeful people whose very presence reminded me that there was life outside of what was going on inside my home. I also got to stay fit, which was a win amidst a sea of losses. "Sure my husband had psychosis, and now I fear he might take his life—but, hey—look! My pants actually fit." As I write this, Joe's mind is clear. My pants no longer fit. I'm still deciding how I feel about this reversal.

The Girl Who Makes It

I am the girl
Who makes it

Who carves
Her life
From stone
With just a chisel
And her will

Who recreates herself
On the fly
Because that
Is what survival
Requires

I am the girl
Who goes
Through hell
And is
Destroyed

Yet
Somehow
Here
I am

Her World Went Black

And once again
Her world went black

And the darkness
She feared most
Returned

But then
She remembered
All she had learned
In the dark

She remembered that she knew how to find light again

She remembered not to wait on others to give light

She remembered how to get the light back

So that's exactly
What she did

MARRIAGE SURVIVAL

How does a marriage survive this? I honestly don't know.

It's almost not survivable.

Two things, though:

- I'm not sure why I stayed.
- I'm glad that I did.

When we got married, I distinctly remember the contentment of knowing that I had married a jewel of a human being. Someone so good and kind. I remember thinking, no matter how blindness changes our lives, one thing that won't ever change is who my husband is at the core. And that was enough for me. I never anticipated a life of decadence . . . only anticipated a life of simplicity and kindness.

Living with blindness was not a big deal for many years of our marriage. Though it was sad as Joe lost more vision over time, he always adapted. Vision loss did not change his steady, happy demeanor. Mental illness was different. I had no idea mental illness could obliterate the core of a person, at least temporarily. Mental illness made my husband unrecognizable for many years. I mean that literally.

Remember a bit earlier, when I mentioned my husband's first hospitalization—the one where he'd been released to his sister's home because I was still too afraid to be in the same house with him? The one where he ended up back in the hospital just two days after release? There were two days between when he was released and when he got readmitted, in which I had to figure out if I was going to be able to be around him. I knew he couldn't stay with his sister forever, and I had no idea how to make myself unafraid or even if I should. I planned to meet him for the first time one on one at his sister's house. We made plans to go for a walk around the block. I was hesitant to be in his presence, but something about meeting outside in public was comforting to me. When I pulled up to his sister's home, Joe came out to greet me and our beloved Golden Retriever Noble, whom I had brought along for moral support.

Goldens have the reputation of being sweet, loving dogs, and ours was no exception. Noble was eighty pounds of pure love. He was my steady, peaceful companion. He adored everyone.

Yet, on that day, Noble—the only other witness to what happened that morning before police came and removed Joe from our home—did not recognize my husband. He did not greet Joe as if he'd been raised by him for the past seven years. Noble kept his distance. Then showed complete disinterest. He did not recognize my husband. Or maybe he did. Maybe he recognized and remembered. I found Noble's reaction beyond validating because I didn't recognize the version of Joe before me, either.

That day, Joe was soft spoken. Nice enough but flat-toned. His mannerisms were foreign. He walked hunched over with a shuffle. His tone of voice was stilted. There was no lightness to him. His body was still processing a month's worth of heavy hospital medication, which, when combined with the onset of mental-health issues, changed him into a stranger. There was no discussion of the initial event. No remorse. No awareness that our lives had imploded. As we walked around the block, my parents called, and Joe had a brief conversation with them. Joe has very little memory of this day. He doesn't remember the phone conversation with my parents at all. I wish I didn't remember or retain these moments, either. I want to forget them like he has. That he was in such a rough state after all those weeks in the hospital was pretty devasting to me. It was hard not to think that maybe he was permanently changed. It was too early to say what that might mean for our marriage. He ended up re-hospitalized at a new hospital shortly after our visit.

Home

During Joe's first hospitalization, my mother stayed with me for a bit, and then my dog and I moved into my brother's house, happy for the company. Sometimes at night or on weekends, I'd try going home. I had to practice being in our home alone. I had to practice being back in the space where awful memories had just been made. I'd take a shower. Or read the mail. I couldn't stay, though. Our home had always been peaceful. A little oasis. Now every room held painful memories. Our lives would never be the same, and our home only reminded me of that. At first, two hours was the most I could stand. I like to cook and found that using the time to try new recipes helped make the time there tolerable. It took a few weeks for me to build up the courage to move back in. Thankfully, I had Noble to accompany me, and he didn't seem to mind being back home at all. If he could do it, I could, too.

After Joe's admission to that second hospital, eventually the time came for him to be discharged once again. This time the hospital involved me in his release plan. They arranged for us to spend time together so that I felt safe. He was still confused, but he wasn't as scary. His behavior was not threatening. I felt okay about picking him up and bringing him home. Honestly, even if I didn't feel okay about picking him up, it wouldn't have mattered. Hospitals can't keep people until they are well. Eventually Joe had to come home. It was time to pick him up.

It's hard to describe the feeling I had as we drove out of the hospital parking lot. It wasn't happiness. It was more like caution. The person beside me was a mystery. I used to know him better than I knew anyone, and, now, it felt like I didn't know him at all. Despite the fact that he hadn't been home for close to six weeks between the two hospitalizations, I don't think either of us was in a hurry to get home. He mentioned wanting a haircut, so we pulled into a nearby barbershop. I watched this barber happily chatting and clipping away, realizing he had no idea that we were fresh out of a psych ward on our way back to a home that would never be the same. Life is so bizarre.

An hour or so later, we made it home. It was not a happy homecoming. Sad things had happened in this home the last time we were together in it. We walked through each room in our house, trying to overcome the bad memories that had been created. That first night, I made sure he had what he needed. Food. Medications. Etc. At bedtime, I said goodbye and went back to my brother's house for the night. I had done okay being alone with him during the day but was not ready to let my guard down enough to be asleep near him at night.

I remember that Joe's eyes looked so sad when I told him I would not be staying the night. Just as I had been afraid to be in our home alone until recently, Joe was also afraid to stay in our home alone. My heart hurt for him. We were both so very broken, but, that night, I had to choose me. I couldn't stay. He asked if he could keep Noble with him. At that moment, I honestly wasn't sure about Joe's ability to keep himself safe or to keep our dog safe. He was not in any way well. Hospitals don't keep psych patients until they are well. They keep patients until they are medicated enough for minimum function outside of a hospital setting and then leave the rest of the healing to outpatient care. Heavy on my mind was what might happen if a delusion came back and he hurt our dog. I loved my Noble more than life but relented and agreed to leave him there with Joe.

Early the next morning, I left my brother's and drove back home. I remember the relief that washed over me as I opened the door at 7 a.m. to find them both alive. A couple of months earlier, I would never have believed there would be a time when I would not trust my husband to stay alive or keep our dog alive if left alone. Life changes just that quickly.

On night two, I remained in the house with Joe overnight. He slept soundly (medications will do that). I stayed awake all night. And I mean all night. Eyes wide open, lying next to him, willing myself to stay there. Any movement he made sent me into a state of even higher alert, as I kept one eye on him and another on the canister of mace sitting inches from me on the bedstand. At times, I picked it up and held it with me in the bed, vowing never to be taken by surprise again.

Romantic, huh?

You Can't Know

Unless
You've picked
Your spouse up
From a mental hospital
At least
A couple
Of times
You can't know

Unless
You've driven directly
From the hospital
To the barber
Or to a restaurant
To delay
The going home
You can't know

Unless
You've had to practice
Standing peacefully
In each room
Of your house
To erase
The memories
Made there
You can't know

Unless
You've sat with him
Hours, weeks, months

Marriage Survival

During confusion
You can't know

Unless
You've kept
Both of you
Afloat
While you waited
For confusion
To lift
You can't know

Unless
You've felt the chill
Of seeing
I Give Up
In his eyes
Yet again
You can't know

Unless
You've sat
Extra minutes
In your driveway
Gathering courage
Afraid this
Might be the day
He's done it
You can't know

You can see
The very tip
Of the massive iceberg
Underneath

You can catch
The faintest
Glimpses

But unless
You're the one
It's happening to
You really
Just can't
Know

Damage

I wonder sometimes
What long-term damage
He will have
From the medicines
He takes
To help him

I wonder sometimes
What long-term damage
I will have
From carrying
This much sadness inside
For this long

Neither is optional

But I do wonder sometimes
About these things
Which are
Permanently
Changing us
Both
From the inside out

Impact

If you want to know how mental illness impacted our marriage, this is it. Our sweet, happy marriage was replaced by a marriage based on fear, lack of trust, and illness management.

Our marriage for the next four years was not a partnership. It was one of patient and caretaker.

Every ounce of Joe's energy was put toward healing his own mind and surviving. It had to be this way. Every ounce of my energy was put toward helping him heal and survive.

There was no give and take. It was all give. What I needed or wanted did not matter. My fears did not matter. Well, actually they did matter and were acknowledged during my weekly therapy sessions. But in our marriage, how this situation was impacting me was not on the table for discussion. If I tried to bring up how hard this whole turn of events was on me, my words were met with silence. Not an angry silence. It was more that Joe couldn't process any deep feelings . . . his own or mine. He had no capacity for empathy. He was a shell.

My dog didn't recognize him. I didn't recognize him. The core of him was gone.

The husband I loved was gone.

The husband I lived with during those four years was not a person I would have chosen to marry.

Not a person I would have dated.

Not a person I would have spoken with at a party (that line is funny because I don't really do parties anyway).

Not a person I would have committed my life to.

Not a person I would have admired for his kindness.

Not a person I could share a laugh with.

Yet here he was.

As it turned out, he wasn't really gone. He was just hidden. Deeply hidden. Almost forever hidden. Buried underneath pain, illness, and broken dreams.

Separate Together

Before mental illness, we were two people but lived like one. We were completely in sync. We spent most of our time together and liked it that way. After work, we walked our dog almost daily on a local trail. On weekends, we either spent time together with other couple friends or just hung out at home doing projects or reading. It was easy to be in each other's company.

After mental illness, there was nothing fun or peaceful about our time together. He was barely interested in being alive within our home, so he was definitely not interested in anything that might be happening outside of our home. But I was. I was in pain, but I was also alive.

So I built a life separate from him.

Joe and I had always been connected at the hip. But after a certain point, I realized that, just because he didn't want to live didn't mean I had to give up my life. I began venturing out with friends or alone and felt the peace of being away from my home, away from the negative-energy vortex that threatened to bring me down. Just because he didn't want to go anywhere—ever—didn't mean I couldn't. I learned to leave him—as he lay on the couch asleep by 6 p.m.—and go out, knowing he'd be in the same place when I got home. Or dead. Heartbreaking as it was, the separate life I lived while he was recovering was my oxygen. It was proof that, even if he didn't make it, I would.

On Sunday mornings, I went alone to local parks, coffee in hand, and wrote hundreds of poems about what my life had become. Seeing the words on paper was validating. This was happening to me. I had opinions about it. I was surviving hell. I went from being connected at the hip to Joe to building a life without him. There was something about establishing consistent patterns in the middle of chaos that helped me find my center. It became normal not to have him with me. At one point, I made peace with losing him.

I wanted so much for him to get better. Yet I had no control over if that would happen. I was fairly certain that he would eventually take his own life.

And even if he didn't, I knew that the current state of my marriage was not sustainable. During the horrible first few months of mental illness, I remember thinking, *If someone told me that I'd get my husband back if I could just hold on for a certain amount of time, what amount of time would be reasonable?* My first thought was three years. I could live this hell for three years if I knew I'd get Joe back at the end. So that's what I was trying to do.

The problem was, we were in year four. Time was running out. The sadness he carried within him spread everywhere in our home, and it was suffocating. I needed air. I did not sign up to live out the rest of my one precious life with someone who didn't want to live. But what kind of person leaves her blind, mentally ill husband?

Apparently, almost *this* kind of person.

I called our local housing authority and found out that blind people qualify for subsidized housing in our town. I asked them to send me an application. I started filling it out. I left it half-filled in my desk drawer. I liked knowing it was there. I liked knowing that if I needed out of this marriage, he would have a place to live. We owned our house together, but I had no intention of leaving it.

In many ways, I had already lost him. He was still alive, but he was dead inside. I wasn't sure how many years of living like this I had in me. I knew I didn't have many more but took comfort in thinking about how all this might end.

And This Is How It Ends

And this is how it ends

He steps up, manages this disease, and lives a splendid life
And I live it with him, or

He is unable to manage this disease and ends his life
And I survive, move forward,
cherishing the happy years we had, or

He cannot—will not—manage this disease
and lives a long, sad life
And I leave, and go on to live a long, happy life

These are the only options

This does not end with me living a long, sad life

That is not an option

No matter
What happens
To him

What happens
To me
Ends
With happiness

There were years of this. So many years.

Depression Stew

You know
What it's like
To walk into
A home
Where something's
Been simmering
All day

Maybe beef stew
In a Crockpot
Or Italian sauce
On the stove

The scent
Fills the home
Envelops all
Who enter

Depression
Is like that, too

The scent
When you enter
The home
Of someone
Who's simmered
All day
In sadness

A distinct
Texture
In the air

A face
Imprinted
With sleep

A mind foggy, disengaged

The unmistakable
Disheartening
Scent of it

Depression stew

I never said these words out loud to him.
But I think he heard them loud and clear.

Choose

Choose life or
Choose death

But don't stay here
In the middle
Of nowhere
Suffering

You can't

I can't

It's too much

Just
Choose

The reality of disability in marriage was so much harder than I thought it would be. The kind of hard that onlookers in our younger days probably realized was coming but that we were blissfully unable to imagine.

"Magic" was written when the fairy dust in our marriage had disappeared and describes the reality of living with a disabled spouse who had given up.

Magic

Any magic
In my house
Is there
Because
I bring it

Nothing done
That I don't do

No plans made
That I don't make

Nothing dreamed
That I don't dream

No magic other
Than what
I bring

No magic
Lives here

Just a tired
Magic maker

We all love stories about heroic disabled people who defy the odds. Who not only overcome but also have a positive attitude while doing the overcoming. But what about all the other disabled people?

"Exceptions" is what it is like to live with a disabled spouse who is not heroic or admirable—who is just surviving. Honestly, who is human.

Exceptions

We only
Hear about
The exceptions

Disabled people
Who are
Exceptional

The Jonis
The Bocellis
The blind mountain climbers
The limbless Olympians

I realize now
I only ever heard
About the exceptions
The admirably disabled

I never thought to wonder
Where were the others?
Where were the unexceptional?

The angry ones

The ones
Who can't

Make peace
With their loss

The ones
Who would rather die
Than live
A limited life

The ones
Too sad
To try

I know now
That the exceptional
Are few

And I know now where
The unexceptional are

I know
Where one is
Anyway

I know now
That the disabled
Who suffer
Are hidden away

Struggling through life
Battling through loss

The majority

But out of view
And in many ways
Alone

NO ONE TELLS YOU

I wasn't prepared for mental illness. I didn't know the common early signs. I didn't know how quickly things could go bad. I had no idea what getting help would entail. I didn't realize the role shame would play.

I didn't know these things because people don't talk about mental illness.

I wasn't prepared. But I want you to be prepared in case this ever happens to someone you love. So, here, I will talk frankly. This section is for anyone who has not yet experienced a loved one having an episode of mania or psychosis but will. And that right there is the first thing that's hard. You can't tell ahead of time who will experience mental illness in this lifetime. It could be your loved onc. It could be you.

In an ideal world, help would swoop in and link those struggling with mental illness to effective treatment well before mania or psychosis ever had a chance to take hold.

But in order for that to happen,

people would need to know what the early confusing signs of
mental illness look like
in day-to-day life.
But in order for people to know the early signs,
people who have gone through or witnessed manic or

psychotic episodes already
would need to reveal some of the behaviors that
their sick loved ones displayed.
Behaviors that can be shocking and
devasting when seen for the first time.

You can imagine why people don't openly share that information. You can imagine wanting to fiercely protect your own recovering loved-one's reputation and opting not to share such delicate details openly.

I wish I had known a lot more about the early signs of mental illness. I wish I had known that fast talking and circular logic were signs of mania. I wish I had known that it's possible for someone in the middle of a mental-health crisis to go effortlessly back and forth between making paranoid statements and perfectly sensible statements. I wish I had known that the end game to this escalating mania and paranoia was going to be a much-scarier psychosis. But who was ever going to tell me that?

Here are some things that no one tells you.

No One Tells You About the Early Signs

When the first signs that something wasn't right with Joe began to appear, my initial reaction was to try to rationalize his actions and statements. I had no reason to think that he could be having a mental-health crisis. Then again, I didn't know what a mental-health crisis even looked like. I didn't jump to that conclusion when he talked non-stop because, even though his speech had more intensity to it, he had always been a chatty person. I was aware that his words weren't his typical funny or insightful observations about life. They were more his strong opinions about how he thought the world worked and how we needed to be on guard in case the world got crazier than it already was. The world was a bit nuts at the time, so I wasn't too surprised that he was having feelings about it. I don't know what the world will look like by the time you are reading these words, but, even now, as I write, this world is a mess. There is a lot to be scared of.

So it wasn't abnormal back then to be concerned about the state of the world, just as it isn't now. I also wasn't super concerned when I woke up one morning to find him already wide awake, even though that was a role reversal for us. I had always been a lover of early mornings, no stranger to getting up to catch a sunrise, and typically the first one up to start most days. But that day, not only was he wide awake—he hadn't slept. That was odd. And yet I wasn't concerned until it happened the next night as well.

His incessant talking gained momentum and started to feel like a freight train of words. The words just kept coming, and I couldn't get out of their path. His speech got more intense and began to focus on anything and everything about the Catholic church. He was expressing more than just a passionate opinion. His tone was angry. He was growing more and more agitated by the minute. It took a few days for me to see it clearly, but with the constant talking, the lack of sleep, and hyperfocus on the Catholic Church, I began to realize that something was really off.

I look back on this short period of days now, and it's a bit embarrassing. How did I not know right away? All I can tell you is that the odd behaviors kind of sneak up on you. I was busy going about my normal life, with no reason to suspect Joe was heading into crisis. The time period from when I first noticed his fast talking to the day he was taken from our home in restraints was approximately two weeks. His most intense, sleepless, and agitated behaviors happened during the final three days of that two-week span.

Two days before the police came was when I started to really worry about him. His intensity was annoying to me. But he also seemed scared. Tortured internally. I didn't know yet that it was mental health. I just knew that it wasn't normal. I wanted to sit down and cry and also to run away because no one had ever told me what to do in a situation like this.

No one ever tells you what to do when:

1. A husband's words become gibberish and increasingly paranoid
2. A loved one insists on describing a reality unlike anything you know to be real
3. Your spouse claims she is God
4. Your relative, in all seriousness, advises you to stay away from specific people because they are aliens
5. Your sibling does something so jaw-droppingly bizarre in public that you can't even form words to respond

If you have no point of reference for mental illness, you have no idea what you are seeing—much less any idea what to do next. It's everything awful, especially the first time you witness this type of behavior. Later on, once you realize that these bizarre behaviors are textbook-common signs of mania or psychosis, it's still awful. But it's more familiar. You figure out how to function despite what you are feeling. Despite what you are seeing.

No One Tells You That It's Scary

No one tells you that untreated mania can lead to psychotic behavior, which is truly one of the scariest things you can ever witness.

Before I go on, I do want to say that, in my experience, most mental illnesses do not make a person do scary things. In fact, if a person around you is struggling with a mental-health issue such as anxiety or depression or even delusion or schizophrenia, you likely won't ever know. These are usually personal battles fought privately and bravely. In the vast majority of cases—especially when talking about individuals who are in or have had successful treatment (e.g., therapy, medication)—the advice "Don't be scared of people with mental illness" is perfectly reasonable.

But there are exceptions, and I know that only because I lived one.

When it comes to untreated severe mental illness, I think sometimes fear is a perfectly acceptable response. Individuals in the grip of mania or psychosis interpret reality differently. They often demonstrate an astounding lack of judgment or self-awareness during these episodes, because these conditions can make reality appear to be something that it is not. As a result, bad things happen. Boundaries are broken, families are torn apart, marriages are ruined, and dreams are dismantled—and that's just for starters. Untreated mental illness is heartbreak. Sometimes you should be afraid.

When I hear people downplaying the scariness of talking to someone with a mind confused by mania or psychosis, it feels insulting and untruthful to me. Untreated mental illness isn't something to take lightly. It is scary, and it can be dangerous. It doesn't mean that the people going through it are bad people. It means that they are sick people.

Joe was terrifying when he was experiencing psychosis. He was sure that the world worked exactly as his broken mind was telling him it did. He was loud. Screamy. Paranoid. Bossy. Amped up. He was talking constantly and in circles, meaning he thought he was making great points about how religion worked and how the Bible should be interpreted, but I couldn't, for the life of me, understand what his point was. So I'd ask him to explain again, but it never got clearer. He got louder and louder but never clearer. Joe's mania escalated to psychosis. He began claiming that he now understood the Bible completely but more importantly, he said that he believed he was God.

Because that apparently wasn't disturbing enough, this is also when the paranoia kicked in. He decided that a few friends of ours were not safe and said we should stay away from them. He repeated random numbers over and over, telling me they were significant and that only he could understand why. He would talk and then unexpectedly break into laughter, but nothing was funny. He laughed like someone who had made a great discovery might laugh. Like how someone who had an epiphany and now understood the whole Bible might laugh. Because that's what he thought was happening. He thought he all of a sudden had great wisdom, and he was thrilled.

Except when he wasn't thrilled.

He woke me up from sleep telling me we were in danger but couldn't explain from what. I spent hours trying to get him to help me understand what he was saying and feeling. In the twenty-three years I'd known him up until that point, he had always been logical. I was trying to give him the benefit of the doubt. I was trying to get logic from a mind incapable of logic at that moment. It's really scary to be in the presence of someone whose mind is malfunctioning in real time. It's equal parts terribly devastating and deeply disturbing.

I had never been exposed in person to this kind of broken-minded behavior before. My only point of reference for such disturbing behavior was the scary movies I'd watched as a kid, where the mass murderer was always a nonsensical crazy man. Joe was not a mass murderer, but he was playing the part of crazy man very convincingly. The closest I'd come to being around such unpredictability in person was when I was with people who were behaving or speaking oddly because they were drunk. Somehow, that scenario was a bit more charming because I knew the behavior would end in a few hours. There is nothing charming about psychosis, though. I wished so badly that there was a clear root cause. Wished the confusion could simply be slept off, bringing about a clear mind in the morning. It's not that way, though. Mental illness at this level can't be slept off. It requires treatment. Fortunately for us and the people we love, treatment exists.

No One Tells You About the Shock

It's hard to put into words the shock of witnessing someone's brain actively misfiring. I remember feeling like I was watching it happen but also feeling like I wasn't really there. I wasn't sure what was happening, but I knew it was bad. I could not reconcile the words and behaviors I was seeing with who I knew Joe to be. Joe's disturbing behaviors were devastating for me to witness—but not at all out of the ordinary in terms of how people typically act during psychosis. I didn't have that information yet, though. I was witnessing something I didn't have words for. The words existed. I just hadn't been exposed to them yet.

I also wasn't prepared for the shame I felt that this was happening. His behaviors just before he was first hospitalized were embarrassing, socially unacceptable. Did I mention that psychosis and nakedness sometimes go hand in hand? Nope, I didn't. That's because it's embarrassing. I'll spare you the naked psychosis stories, but let's just say that the only thing that disturbed me more than trying to talk to my husband during psychosis was trying to talk to my naked husband during psychosis. These are memories I'd rather not have, but no one asked my opinion on what memories I'd like to retain. So, lucky me—these memories are all mine. These memories taught me that it's impossible to witness such changes in a loved one and not be changed yourself.

No One Tells You That Getting Help Early Is Hard

Maybe no one talks openly about how to get help early because the truth is that entrance into the mental-health system is incredibly difficult. The waitlists are absurd, which just goes to show how many people are struggling with this thing that no one talks about. When you start calling around for an appointment with a therapist to help get your loved one's thoughts clear, it will likely be weeks before an open appointment is available. And finding a psychiatrist will probably take just as long, which is sad, because most psychiatrists won't prescribe medicine unless a therapist is in place. Often, by the time you know a loved one needs help, that loved one does not have weeks to spare before becoming acute. They have days, maybe hours. No one tells you that none of this is your fault. No one tells you that sometimes you won't be able to get your loved one help in time.

No One Tells You About Hospitals

No one tells you that if you *do* make it to the hospital for an assessment, it won't be warm and welcoming. It will be cold and lonely. No one tells you that staff will look at you unimpressed as you explain your loved one's disturbing behavior. No one tells you that you will wait there for 8+ hours and will very likely be sent home with a delusional and demented loved one and an unrealistic plan for follow-up help (call a therapist and get yourself some help). No one tells you that not being able to get your loved one help is a secondary trauma. That, as a loved one, you have to stuff your feelings down again and again, because there is no time to process this much loss. That you will have to walk around carrying not only the burden of your loved one's illness but also a heaviness that feels like failure but can't possibly be, because you're doing all you can. No one tells you that the hospitals' first loyalty is to the insurance companies who pay them.

No one tells you that your loved one has to be far beyond what you would normally think of as crisis level for a hospital to admit. Even during the crushing ER visit where Joe outright stated that he was there because he was God, the hospital informed me they would be sending him home. It wasn't until Joe added that he felt unsure about the ability to keep himself or others safe that they admitted him. So, note to self: God will be sent home with you but not the version of God that might hurt self or others.

No one tells you how devastating it is to watch your loved one try to hide his paranoia from hospital admission staff. No one tells you what it feels like to watch your loved one stay brilliantly silent—not because he is sane, but because he thinks the hospital is the enemy. As I sat beside Joe in yet another ER waiting room, he whispered, "I'm not going to say anything, and, then, when we get home, I can explain everything." I sat quietly, with zero fight left in me, hoping that hospital staff would decide that the things Joe wasn't hiding were reason enough for admission. Luckily, we were at a good hospital that day. The staff saw through his plan and admitted him.

No One Tells You About Safety

No one tells you that it's critical to think of ways to protect yourself—your physical self, your finances, and even your reputation—while your loved one is acute. Joe was in and out of hospitals a lot that first year. After each hospital release, he was better but not good. His brain was not clear. He was not scary, but his words were unpredictable. He was teetering on the edge of paranoia, and it was hard to know if he'd tip toward wellness or back into confusion. We had shared an email address for many years, but, when mental illness entered our lives, I took that opportunity to create a separate email for myself. I also changed passwords on our bank accounts and any other accounts that mattered. I took precautions, bought mace, and came up with a plan in case psychosis returned. I was not going to be taken by surprise again. I was hoping for his healing but planning for relapse. I had seen too much. I knew now that hospitals—though doing the best they can—often release mentally ill people long before they are ready. It happens all the time, and, once you walk out of the hospital doors, you are on your own.

No One Tells You About Aftercare

No one tells you that, if you are lucky enough to get a loved one hospitalized, the hospital's job is to stabilize but not to heal. No one tells you that your loved one will be pumped with the heaviest drugs available to begin the process of shutting down all symptoms of insanity, which will result in also shutting down everything recognizable about your loved one's personality. No one tells you that once they are released for outside treatment, your loved one may be lower-level delusional for months as the brain heals and med combinations are tried. No one tells you that the hospital's two-week aftercare program is not nearly long enough to ensure stability. No one tells you how exhausting it is to arrange for others to be present with your loved when you can't because the risk of him acting on suicidal impulse or forgetting to take the medicine that keeps him clearheaded is real, though not real enough for hospitals or insurance companies to deal with.

No One Tells You About the Devastating Search for Providers

No one tells you it may take at least three tries to find the right therapist, the same to find a compassionate psychiatrist, and six or more tries and many months to find the right mix of medication. No one tells you that, if you stay with your loved one, your life for the next few years will revolve around psychiatric appointments, co-pays, and heartbreak.

No One Tells You About the Guilt

No one tells you that later—when you can feel feelings again—you will feel overwhelming guilt about not getting help sooner. Either because you didn't know the signs or, because *despite* all of the signs, access to mental-health care is ridiculous. No one tells you that you will sit on your bathroom floor and weep out of frustration for how impossible this all is. No one tells you, *Don't beat yourself up for not realizing how sick your loved one was.* The confusion of this disease is that it can be well hidden, and not every delusional person is delusional in every topic. No one tells you that it's confusing because your loved one can be going to work every day, mowing the lawn, and preparing dinners all the while 100% convinced he has special powers that others are not evolved enough to understand. No one tells you that it's so much easier to see how sick someone is when the sickness has overtaken them, and that is why help is usually sought when it's almost too late. That is why getting help often involves the police and involuntary admissions to psychiatric wards. Or at least that's what it involved for us.

No One Tells You About Relapse

No one tells you about the cold shock that hits when—despite best efforts—you realize that your loved one is going over the edge again. No one tells you that it's possible to be both functional and numb as you scramble to get a loved one hospitalized again. No one tells you about the tenuous dance of conversation with someone in a fragile state of mind, the massaging of the other's terrifying broken logic as you attempt to convince a loved one that getting into the car with you and going to the hospital is a good idea. No one tells you that that the chilling words exchanged between you and your delusional loved one during that very hospital ride are ones your loved one won't remember later but that you will never forget. No one tells you that this is one of many reasons you will later require a skilled therapist's help to process these words and EMDR therapy to ensure that the memories are kept at a safe distance so that you can continue to function.

No One Tells You About Losing Friends

No one tells you that it's okay to decide not to share the ugliest details with friends and family because you are holding out hope that your loved one will someday recover and when he does, he is going to need people in his life, and no one would stay if they knew the details. No one tells you about the delicate balance between sharing information with those who ask versus protecting your loved one's privacy. No one tells you how many secrets you will hold because there isn't another choice. No one tells you that many friends won't understand and that more will disappear, and, seriously, it's okay. Just let them go, because mental illness is part of your life now, and you will need strong friends who can handle this shit.

Maybe We Can Start

No one shares the brutally hard details about walking through mental illness with a loved one, because so much of it is painful, embarrassing, scary, and unexplainable.

But maybe we can change that.

Maybe we can start by being honest about what mental illness really looks like.

Maybe we can work on better describing the paralyzing shock of the first event so that it's not so unfamiliar.

Maybe we can work on giving people tools they can use to help loved ones get help.

Maybe we can tweak the mental-health system a bit or in its entirety, so that help is more accessible.

Maybe we can tell HIPAA to go to hell, so admissions staff will make an effort to get an accurate account of behaviors from family members before they make a decision to send a sick person home.

Maybe Progress

Maybe we can make progress. Maybe someday—in the not-too-distant future—we will hear about people who witnessed their first mental-health crisis and, instead of crumbling, recognized the symptoms, took a breath and said to themselves:

Yes, this is shocking.

Yes, my loved one's words and actions are devastating.

But I know what this is, and I know what to do.

I know this isn't personal.

I know this is an illness, and I can be helpful now, just as this person would do for me if the roles were reversed.

But this won't happen unless we talk openly about what mental illness can look like. And we don't talk openly, because shame lingers even in a recovered person. And we don't share our recovery journeys because they are not a straight line.

We don't talk about the hard details of mental illness because the recovered people still need to someday be able to get jobs and meet new friends without carrying the baggage of how they behaved when their minds were broken.

We don't talk about it, but we should.

And I'm trying.

NOVEMBERS

The holiest of all holidays are those
Kept by ourselves in silence and apart
The secret anniversaries of the heart

~Henry Wadsworth Longfellow

The day Joe first broke was November 9, 2011. That day changed me. Even now, the approach of it on the calendar each year hurts. Life continues on around me as it should. Most people have forgotten the date. It is mine alone to remember and honor. And that I do. I typically take that day off from work to free up time for the full weight of my feelings. I take myself somewhere quiet. Always in time for the sunrise. Typically to the beach. With a nice latte. And a journal. Most years I bring my dog, though my OG Noble has long since passed. I sit for hours. I think, write, cry. I mourn it all, every bit of the loss.

I am forever changed. It doesn't matter that so many years have passed and life is now better and happier. It doesn't matter that Joe no longer struggles with confused or suicidal thoughts. Or that he has graduated from college and has steady work that he enjoys. Or that he is stable, happy, and well. Despite all this, a part of me will always expect the worst. Recently, I pulled up to my house and, from my car, noticed that a note had been taped to the front door. My blood went cold and stayed that way until I could get to the door and see that it was a nice note with a milk bone attached to it for my dog. It was a gift from a sweet little neighbor girl. It was not a suicide note confirming that I'd missed the signs once again and that Joe was inside, dead.

Seem extreme? Mental-health issues entered our life just that shockingly. I expect nothing less if they return, though I tell myself I know the signs of mental distress now and can get help earlier. Joe has done a lot of healing. I don't dwell on the possibility of relapse, but I'd be a fool not to consider it. Either way, there is no going back to the days of not knowing that mental-health issues exist.

I lost so much that day that I will never get back. So, on the anniversary of that day, I let myself feel deeply. After the beach, sometimes I walk around and visit cute shops. Or go to a park. Or sometimes a movie. I am gentle with myself. I ask no one's permission for honoring the day this way. I used to softly mention the significance of this day to those around me, but my voice was maybe too soft. And it ended up hurting more trying to explain why the day might still hurt all these years later. So, I stopped talking about it and instead tucked it deep into my soul. This day is mine to honor.

When I feel up to it, I try to capture what I'm feeling about the day in writing. Really, the whole season is hard for me. Not just the day. But it heals me to put my pain into words. Makes it real. Validates the depth of my pain and the progress I've made through the years.

Fall

Fall
When everything fell
Leaves
Life

It's no wonder
I don't like you
Anymore

Journal Entry—November 2014

I'm weird during this season. I admit it. I'm embracing it. If anyone asks me what my problem is, I'll tell them this:

September

I used to have a
 Nice dog
 Nice marriage
 Nice church
 Nice life

So, in September, I mourn the loss of how simple my life was. I mourn the memory of what contentment felt like. I remember how much I used to look forward to the beautiful colors of the Fall. I remember how happy I was driving down Baldpate Road feeling like I was in a bowl of Fruity Pebbles. I mourn simple joy.

October

I remember walking on the trail, listening to him try to explain how close he felt to God. Listening—not overly concerned, just trying to understand.

I remember half-listening to him on Halloween as we gave out candy, with him in the background trying to tell me his latest thoughts on God.

So, in October, I remember the beginnings of confusion, and I dread the coming of Halloween and the change to November. I mourn the days of feeling like I was a good reader of people. I mourn the days of thinking we are all weird at times . . . we all go through stages, and it passes.

November

I remember intense, confusing walks, confusing discussions during dinner. I remember him giving away his guitar. I remember bronchitis.

No words

November 9th

The beginning of a
Long process of
Losing everything
First Husband
Then God
Then Self
Then Friends

So, in November, I remember how everything was taken from me in such a short time, how devastating the mental-health system is, how I never knew it could hurt to breathe. I mourn taking mental stability for granted. I mourn thinking life was hard but manageable. I mourn the awareness of how dark life is.

Three Years Out

I have a new understanding of God
I have a new sense of self
I have a version of my husband
I have a handful of friends

I mourn my losses
I am proud of my strength
I wonder about my future

Get-Through-It Strategies

I am on emotional lockdown for the season.

If I were a house, there would be iron bars on every window and two pit bulls at the door.

I am extremely vulnerable right now. To tone. To feeling invisible. To feeling alienated. To being asked to share things I'd rather not talk about. To being drawn out and judged.

So, all are at arm's length. No one is getting in, and I'm not coming out.

It's the only way I can establish some sense of safety.

While I'm in here, I will care for myself. I will tell myself how proud I am of me. I will peek my head out and love in ways that are not threatening to me. And I will rest. And waste time. And disappear for as long as it takes to feel secure.

Journal Entry—November 2015

Remember

I'm sad
Because of what
I remember

I remember
His odd eyes
Manic smile
Deep voice
Inches from my face
Screaming threats

I remember
Police asking
If we owned
A gun
My answer: No
And the words
Because he's threatened
To take a gun
And shoot his
Pretty little wife's
Face off

I remember
The paramedic's question
Ma'am, what is he on?
My response: Nothing
And the question again,

No, really—tell us what
He is on

I remember later thinking
I only wish
This was caused

By something
He was on—
Not something
That he is

I remember
White sheets
And restraints
And a gurney with
My naked, screaming husband

Being loaded
Into the ambulance

I remember neighbors
Standing with me
Watching

I remember
The emergency room
Hours later
My screams, and nurses
Pulling him off me
When he grabbed me
From his bed
And wouldn't let go

Novembers

I remember
He left bruises

I remember whole years
Of pain since then
In detail

I remember it all
And wonder
How I am still
Sleeping next to him

Next to someone
Who can turn
Into someone like that
Without medicine

I remember it all
Without fear now

Only sadness
That there is so
Very much
To remember

Never Over

Today
Four years out

It struck me

Why this anniversary
Of hurt

Hurts
So much

It's not the remembrance
Of a day
Long ago
When pain came
And then ended

It's the remembrance
Of the day
That the life we had
Changed

A remembrance
Of being introduced
To a hurt
That will forever
Be part
Of our lives

It's never over

That's the point
That's the source of the pain

The knowledge that
From that day forward
This is forever
And never
Over

Journal Entry—November 2017

The past few weeks I have found myself mentally spent, exhausted, hopping into bed at 7:30 p.m., not wanting to do much. And then the thoughts of: *Why can't I be more on top of things? Why am I not more prepared for the holidays? Why—no matter what the plan is on Thanksgiving—do I not want to do it? Why do I just feel like hibernating?* And I actually thought for a few days, *Wow! What is wrong with me?*

Good golly—what is wrong? Did I really have to ask myself? And then I remembered: This is how these months *always* go. It just snuck up on me this year because we had been busy preparing to share our story for the first time as part of "This Is My Brave" (side note to reader: Look this organization up—it's amazing), which brought a new level of acceptance. I guess the distraction is good. It was a nice relief not to be specifically dreading this season—to have it pushed to the side so much so that, when I *did* start feeling sad, I had to ask myself, *Why?*

So, I guess some seasons will be like this.

I will either be fully aware and braced for the pain.

Or the pain will sneak up on me.

Either way, I don't ever foresee a painless Fall. That would be somewhat absurd.

Let Myself Remember

Mostly I move forward
Walk gently
Live open
Without fear

Despite all
That I
Have been through

But on this day
I stop

I let myself remember

All of it

Every painful detail

On this day
I allow myself
To feel
The full depth
Of what
I lived through

I do this
To honor
Me

To show my pain
Well-deserved
Respect

I do this
Because I survived
The unthinkable

I did that

I made it

And while I'm
Not one
To sit and dwell

This day
Is sacred

Set aside

To let myself
Remember
The pain

A difficult practice
Perfected in solitude

That also
Reminds me clearly
Of my strength

Happier

Maybe
I should
Be happier

Because he is making
Great strides

Because he is getting
Things done

Because he is showing up more
For his life

For our life

Maybe
I should
Be happier

But really
I'm just tired
From holding it all
For so long

Really
I'm just waiting
To see how this goes

To see if it will continue

And to figure out
What to do
If it doesn't

Journal Entry—November 2020

I do believe this is the first season in nine years that I have not been weighed down and distracted by pain. I still feel pain, but the edges aren't as sharp. I still feel sadness, but I don't feel overtaken by it.

This is progress.

This is healing, though healing doesn't mean unchanged.

This season . . .

I am still taking November 9th off from work

I can't help but think that speaking as part of the CIT program (a Crisis Intervention Training program for law enforcement that invites family members to share mental-health experiences) has possibly been the final shedding of shame around this experience. Speaking, being heard, offering up the experience to others, and having it add value to their work—this makes me feel free.

Instead of dreaming of surviving the season . . .

I am thinking maybe I could do something actually fun on November 9th.

Maybe I could have joy on that day instead of exhaustion from coming up with ways to outrun the pain.

I still love sunrises . . . still will try to find one . . . still will stop and breathe and feel.

But the load I am carrying is lighter.

I am thankful.

Bad-Day Reliever

At the beginning, every minute of every November 9th was so incredibly painful that I needed to find tangible ways to put good into the day. I did this by putting coffee shop gift cards on random people's cars. The gift cards included an anonymous note explaining that I was honoring a hard anniversary in my life by putting good out into the world and hoping I would brighten the receiver's day. Since the painful event took place in my town, it was important to me to leave the gift cards only on cars in my town—an attempt to exchange the negative energy of those memories for the positive ones being created.

I loved the randomness of selecting a recipient's car: one time at the grocery-store parking lot, another on a random side street, once near the library, another time at the park-and-ride, etc. That part of the morning always gave me special happiness. The thrill of walking up to someone's car before sunrise and putting a gift card under the windshield wiper was the perfect way to start a hard day. I always snapped a quick picture to memorialize where I left that year's card. I was also always slightly panicked about the thought of being caught, half expecting a car alarm to go off . . . something that never happened.

Throughout the day, as the pain came close while I sat on the beach in peaceful silence, the thought of the person finding a card on their car made me smile inside. I secretly hoped that whoever found it would treat themselves to a latte. For all the pain in the world, there will also be random joyful surprises. I needed to believe that for myself, so I made that a reality for others.

The intense pain of this day stayed with me for years. It wasn't until six years later—after I'd told my story publicly for the first time as part of This Is My Brave—that I noticed a shift in the pain's intensity. The day still hurt badly, but it was less severe. I had shared my story with the world so that I didn't have to carry so much of it in my body. It was the beginning of feeling that I didn't need to outrun the pain anymore. Having my story and experience honored by more than just myself had lifted some of the weight.

I'll never fully get over what happened. It will always be a part of me. And the pain I carry is not something I feel compelled to explain or justify. It just *is*. Still, having my story heard and having it help others in the grip of pain—this has lightened the burden I carry. And in the open space that is left, even on this most painful day, it is a pleasant surprise to realize that there is room now for happiness, too.

BAD ADVICE I HAVE RECEIVED

As much as I don't love when talk of mental-health issues is met with silence, I get it. A lot of people are afraid to say the wrong thing, and it definitely hurts when wrong things are said. Here are some of the most painful comments that came my way when I was already in a fair amount of pain. I am hopeful that, as the world learns more about what it's like to experience mental-health issues, the advice offered will be a bit more thoughtful.

"Many who experience psychosis never recover"

~ said to me forty-eight hours after the event, when my husband was still hospitalized and acutely delusional, and I was still in shock. Would we ever—as non-medical professionals—show up in the waiting room of an ER and tell a family whose loved one was just in a terrible car wreck that "most people in this type of accident won't make it"? This type of unsolicited input is the opposite of comforting.

"Don't tell anyone about this"

~ said to me three weeks after the event, while my husband was still hospitalized and while life felt plenty alone enough already. These words only reinforced the message that mental-health issues are shameful, encouraged me to isolate, and made me question reaching out for help from the people in my life who loved me. Also, for the record—I've told *everyone.*

"I went to visit him and played him worship music. He was really into it. God has done a miracle and healed him"

~ said to me a week after the event, by a well-meaning-but-clueless evangelical who visited him in the hospital but with complete disregard for the fact that Joe had been admitted for religious psychosis. That visit—which served only to feed Joe's delusions—taught me that people will see only what they want to see. And it taught me that I needed to protect my husband not only from himself but also from people on the outside who might do more harm than good.

"He should have told me. Why wasn't he honest with me?"

~ yelled into my overwhelmed ear via phone by one of Joe's first therapists, while I stood in the ER, waiting for Joe to be admitted for suicidality. This was Joe's third hospitalization, and I knew that, if the ER had Joe's most updated therapy records, it would help them determine next steps. So I called his therapist to make the request. Instead, I got to endure being berated over the phone I was holding in one hand, while my other hand was holding Joe's, whose anguish at that point was causing him severe physical pain. The *blame* angle only added to my pain. Joe had been clearly and obviously suicidal for weeks. It wasn't a surprise to me and shouldn't have been a surprise to the therapist.

"Are you going to leave him?"

~ asked of me over the phone during his first hospitalization, when my wounds were still so fresh, I didn't even remember how to *breathe*—much less hatch a plan to leave. This is when I realized that some of the questions coming my way were going to be more about satisfying a curiosity than helping me.

Better Things to Say

I know that it's hard to find the right words when it comes to mental-health issues. I mean, *really.* What exactly do we want people to say?

- "Happy Suicide Prevention month. I know this month means a lot to you" seems a bit bold.
- "Hey, nice article about your deepest, most personal pain" also seems to fall flat.

It's complicated, isn't it? None of us are practiced in compassionate discussion around mental health. I wish I could take back some of my own past, imperfect attempts at comfort, too. Luckily, we can all learn how to respond well. If you are struggling to find the right words, you can try

"I'm sorry this is happening"

or

"Thank you for trusting me with that"

or

"That seems incredibly hard, and I don't know what to say, but I'll be by your side through whatever comes."

If you are still not sure what to say, just listen, bring someone flowers, or make them their favorite dessert. The simplest responses are usually the best.

THE WAY WE TALK ABOUT IT

We have choices when it comes to the way we talk about mental health. We can create distance and shut down any discussion about mental health. We can also create space for people to speak openly and then make time to listen. Whatever we decide, there is an impact.

Creating Distance

There are so many assumptions about people who experience mental-health issues. When hearing that someone struggles with mental health, it is too easy to make assumptions that create distance, like: *She must have come from a messed-up family* or *He never could handle stress anyway* or *Wasn't that person a drug user?*

Other thoughts might include:

- This happens only to people who are weak
- He must have always been a little off
- This happens only to those with bad DNA
- This happens only to those who have made a series of bad choices
- This should not be shared publicly

- This won't happen to me because I grew up in a strong, loving family
- I care, but I have no idea how to respond to this
- This topic doesn't affect me, so I actually don't care to know more

None of us perfectly understand mental illness. So, some lean into theories that create distance and keep mental-health issues at arm's length. That is much easier than accepting the reality that mental-health struggles are common and can happen to absolutely anyone for no good reason. Creating distance may be comforting, but it is futile.

We don't have to understand everything about mental health to have compassion for the struggle. We don't have to understand it all, but maybe we could work on acknowledging some basics, like:

Mental-health issues exist
They happen to good people
When they happen, they can be difficult to navigate
They can take a while to resolve

Mental-health issues are not a moral failing or a sign of weakness. They are not rare. They are just one of life's many realities, and acknowledging them as such would be a strong start.

Creating Space

If Joe had completed his suicide plan, many people would have been shocked, but I wouldn't have been one of them. It was clear during those years that he was not okay and that he was struggling to find reasons to live. But I didn't talk about this openly with anyone because *How do we even do that?* A few weeks into our mental-health crisis, people in our lives were genuinely compassionate when they asked how Joe was and I shared how badly things were going. A few years into the crisis, if I was ever honest about how hard things still were, the look on people's faces told me all I needed to know about how much to share going forward. My honesty only made them sad. And I was too busy dealing with my own sadness and Joe's sadness to deal with theirs, too.

Maybe they felt guilt that their own lives were still going well. Imagine if you asked someone how they were and they responded: "Actually, pretty bad. Remember that last time we talked? I told you that my house was on fire. Well, my house is still on fire, and, now, it has spread to the barn." Unless you had plans to show up at that house with a hose, it would be really hard to know what to say. In most cases, I learned to respond to any questions about Joe's condition with vague answers. Eventually, people stopped asking. This made people much more comfortable—*other* people—not me. I was still living an extremely anguished life. I just wasn't making other people sad by talking about it.

There is just not a lot of space in our world to talk about ongoing struggles.

We aren't great at talking about our own mental-health struggles, and we aren't great at listening to others talk about them. We struggle to find the right words to describe our experiences, and we struggle to find the right words to say in response. It's complicated.

For example, when we lose people to suicide, they disappear. From the world, yes—but also from our conversation. After such a tragic loss, we don't hear much about what life was like for that person leading up to the suicide. We also don't hear much about what life is like for the loved ones who have to quietly and shamefully mourn their person after a loss. There is shame in speaking about the painful realities leading up to this tragedy, and there is shame around mourning afterwards. Shame all around.

I wish we lived in a world that created safe spaces for difficult topics.

I believe strongly that what we say out loud about someone else's mental-health story will determine how comfortable people are sharing their own mental-health stories with us.

- So if your dear friend and co-worker hears you say, "People who die by suicide are selfish," it's a pretty safe bet that this co-worker—who might also be struggling with suicidal thoughts—won't be confiding in you.
- Likewise, if you say out loud: "Medicine is for weak-minded people," it's fairly certain that your friends who are taking medications are never going to tell you. Strong opinions stated loudly build barriers between us where we need bridges. It's impossible to know a person well when important parts of their lives, like this one, become off limits for discussion. We are all entitled to our opinions, but those closest to us are more likely to share their struggles with us when we express our opinions in a way that creates space for curiosity.

We can do better in the way we talk about mental-health issues and in the way we respond to those who share their own mental-health journeys. We can close the distance by acknowledging that mental-health issues happen to great people. We can create space for people around us to talk openly about mental health. We can do better, and when we do better, those around us will do better, too.

Journeys On but Not Asked For

For the things
That break
Our spirits

For the way
Life goes
Sometimes

For journeys
On but not
Asked for

May peace
Still find you
There

CAPACITY

Engaging people in thoughtful discussions about mental-health issues is hard. People can absorb only so much information on such a difficult topic, especially if the idea is new to them. We can process only what we have the capacity to process, and, while that capacity can expand over time, it can't be rushed. A pint jar can't expand into a gallon jar overnight. When Joe was depressed to the point of suicidal ideation, if I was trying to explain his depression to someone who had no understanding of depression, I would simply say, "Joe is deeply sad right now to the point of not wanting to exist." I wouldn't share that he had been sleeping in the same dirty sweatshirt for weeks, that he slept most hours of the day, that his face was stoic and hard with no trace of life, that he was not kind or that, any day now, I was sure he would kill himself, and I knew exactly how. That would have been too much to share with someone who barely understood what it might be like to feel deeply sad. If you overload people—by trying to dump a gallon's worth of material into a pint-sized jar—all you'll get is overflow and waste.

The good news is that people can expand and grow . . .

So, when introducing mental-health issues into conversation, maybe give those with pint-jar capacity just enough information to fill a pint jar, those with quart-jar capacity just a quart, etc. That way, material is not wasted and can be retained for examination later. The jar can always be traded up when it's comfortably full and they are ready for more information.

For unknown reasons, but sometimes by choice, some people will ever have only pint-jar capacity when it comes to talk about mental health. That's okay, too. In these cases, the best we can do is to make the pint's worth of information offered the very best it can be.

LIFE NOW

Whole

We have been through a lot. It's been exhausting. For a long stretch of years, I was pretty sure things would never be better. We had lost so much, and I could not see a path forward to ever being okay again.

Yet, somehow, here we are today. Whole. We are happy. Life is good again.

Though it took years of stops and starts, countless providers, deep self-evaluation, going back to school for a new career, and a willingness to change the expectations he had of life, Joe found his way back to wellness. He found work that incorporates his old love for music with his passion for helping people who feel lost and now shares his story weekly at local recovery centers. It took four solid years of hell before he found his way back to life, but he made it. He loves his life again. Enough years have gone by with him healthy that I no longer feel like I need to stand guard over his mental wellness. He has become expert in monitoring himself and in doing what he needs to do to stay well. I've watched him rebuild his life in a way that incorporates blindness. I've watched us rebuild our marriage brick by brick in a way that incorporates blindness, several disastrous years of mental health, and new, more-expansive beliefs.

Unasked Questions

When I talk to people about mental health, sometimes I get the sense that there are areas they want to ask in-depth questions about but also don't want to offend. There are many valid questions about mental health that don't have a safe space to land. They are seemingly too personal to ask, but many people want to know the answers. *What is the recovery process like? Does everyone with a mental-health issue have to take medication? What is his official diagnosis? Could he ever relapse and get sick again, or is he good now? Aren't you afraid this will happen again? Can people with mental-health issues ever again be successful in life, have strong relationships, and live well? Was he normal before this happened? Why do you talk so much about mental health?*

Here are answers to some of these questions, based on our experience.

The Recovery Process and Medications

It took a long time for Joe to get well again. He had therapy appointments weekly and psychiatry appointments at least monthly. For the first few years, his confusion and depression got noticeably worse at specific times (e.g., during the Fall and full moons. No—that's not creepy *at all*...), and we had to be more cautious. I don't know that I'd call them *episodes*, though, because we managed them before they got bad. But during those times, we increased his provider appointments and were more intentional about him getting enough sleep. If he wasn't sleeping well, we made sure he had medication on hand to help him do so.

Medication adjustments are a clumsy waltz. Early on, whenever his original medications were decreased, I saw slight changes that made it easier to see how his thoughts during the initial crisis became more free-flowing and eventually ended up scrambled. If I noticed concerning thought processes or tones, we would work with his providers to make things right, which meant a med adjustment or change. There were also seasons when his dosage of medicine was increased for a month or two to get him through a rough time and keep him steady.

I walked on eggshells most every day of those years. It was hard for me determine which of his behaviors were normal and which were signs of relapse. For example, if he accidently overheard a disturbing story on the news and had increased anxiety, was that okay, or was it something that was going to escalate into paranoia? His brain was still healing, and I had to make sure his exposure to anything upsetting was limited. I usually watched the news only when he was sleeping, because, God knows, *I* wasn't sleeping.

When his depression finally lifted, if he dared to laugh hard at anything, I'd literally say, "Wait, are you manic laughing or normal laughing?" This would make us both laugh, but I'd still be half wondering. Once when we attended church a few months after his break, I looked at him mid-service and said, "You don't still think you're God, do you?" He looked right back at me and said, "I don't know—you don't still think you're Santa Claus, do you?" *That* was old, funny Joe pushing through the fog.

Joe learned to look within to figure out if he could also sense changes in his energy, and he got good at self-monitoring. Sometimes I'd say, "Hey, I feel like you are a little more amped up today than usual. Do you feel that, too?" Sometimes, he did. Other times, he didn't. But either way, when he reached a certain level of wellness, we could talk about it. This is what the recovery process looked like for us. Once we had a strong provider team in place, we worked at keeping an eye out for slight changes (for the better *or* the worse) and talking them through to figure out what was normal recovery, as opposed to what might be regression. This work took up pretty much every bit of available emotional energy for many years. It takes a long time to see progress, but it's like Christmas when it comes.

Not everyone with mental-health issues needs medications but if mental-health issues have reached a crisis phase (e.g., hospitalization), it's normal to be on several strong medications until the crisis is alleviated. It's kind of like if you had stomach pain and went to the Emergency Room in agony and were given something strong to alleviate the pain while the doctors did the necessary testing to determine that an infected gallbladder might be the problem. You won't always need that level of painkiller, and, once the root problem is addressed, you might not need a painkiller at all. It's the same with mental health. Once you are out of crisis, the work of getting well can begin, and, sometimes, the medications can be adjusted to a lesser level.

Joe originally needed so many strong medications to function that anything left of his personality was buried under a medication haze. It took a discouragingly long period of time to find just the right regimen—one that would set him free from personality prison but also ensure he continued to heal. I didn't know this before, but brains take a long time to heal. We did finally find what seemed like the perfect med combo, but Joe always had concerns about the long-term impact of these medications and his "someday goal" was to taper off of them altogether. I had respect for his concern about the possible long-term negative consequences of these medications while also respecting that these medications might be the thing enabling him to live a full, happy life. Medications are a fluid part of the mental-health-recovery process, a useful tool and something we keep a steady eye on.

The Diagnosis

There is so much shame attached to mental-health diagnoses. There are so many assumptions about the lives of people who are branded with an unflattering mental-health label (really, are there any flattering ones?). After the full years of hell we've been through, many will find it odd that we never did get a clear diagnosis. Joe fit into pieces of a bunch of categories but not squarely into one. At first, I felt that a clear diagnosis was mandatory so that we could be sure we were pursuing the right treatment and medications. Eventually, with best-guess treatments despite an unclear diagnosis, his symptoms dissipated. Along the way, he went from multiple medications to one. This medication is known to be effective for a whole cluster of diagnoses—some that are scary to think about and some that are pretty generic. It's okay. I made my peace with this prescription because it worked. He got well again. All that angst over diagnosis faded into the background because I had my husband back. That's all any of us really want.

Relapse Thoughts

Joe's therapist once described what happened to Joe as one massive life-changing episode that resulted in ripple effects lasting several years. I very much want for this to be a one-time thing (actually, I would have preferred that it be a "none-time thing," but that ship had sailed.)

But we can't be sure if that's how it will play out in the long run.

Some mental-health issues start in childhood and have consistent patterns over time. Others—like Joe's—start later in life and aren't as clearly defined. Like with any medical condition, there are no guarantees. We have several solid mentally healthy years behind us since the initial episode and all the right supports in place if any symptoms ever were to return. Joe's stability has meant that we have our lives back. We go on vacations, eat our favorite falafel, go to concerts at the community theatre, are regulars at our favorite breakfast place—and it's fun. Joe plays music all the time now. I have time to write and practice guitar again. It's been years since I've had to think hard about Joe's mental health. I believe the worst of it is behind us. But relapse is always a possibility, and that truth is pretty freaking unsettling.

Living Well

We live 100% well now. We have a great marriage, we have steady work, and we've been on some wonderful trips the past few years. We will never again take for granted how nice day-to-day life—without crisis—can be.

Though we live well, it is not with the same sense of freedom that we used to have. It's hard to explain other than to say that the innocence is lost. It's a painful casualty of what we have been through. Living well after a spouse's mental-health crisis is a lot like living well with a spouse who has a physical disability (we apparently hit the jackpot here). I wish he'd never gotten sick. I'm glad he's at a point now where he can enjoy life. There are certain environments—with both blindness *and* mental health—that make things challenging, and we work those out as we go. Most of the time, though, he is okay. We are okay. Life is okay.

Who This Happens to and Why

Joe was consistently happy, easygoing, funny, loving, and kind for the 40-plus years before his brain broke. He was as "normal" as the most normal person you know. We like to think that there will always be a clear reason why this happens to people. For example, it's understandable why veterans who have witnessed extreme trauma experience PTSD. But, for many of us, we just don't know the reason. I'm sure that going blind was part of the trigger for Joe's experience, but a lot of people who lose their vision don't have a mental-health crisis. That this came on out of the blue for us only reinforces to me that this could truly happen to *anyone*.

Before mental-health issues entered our life, I used to think they only happened to certain types of people. I made assumptions that put distance between my nice, cozy life and those struggling with messy mental illness. I had a certain image in mind of who might have mental illness and would think, *Yes, that person was always a bit strange.* This experience has shifted my perspective in a brutal—yet necessary—way. When I think of people with mental-health issues now, I no longer think of the "weirdest" people I know. I think of the *best* people I know. This is because mental illness happened to the best person I know. Think of the most solid person you know. It might be your best friend, your sister, or your spouse. That person could one day experience a mental-health issue. The person staring back at you in the mirror? That person is also not immune from mental-health issues. This is why we need to keep talking about it.

Talking About It

Sometimes people ask me if I'm ever embarrassed to share as much as I do about our mental-health experience. My answer is, "Of course." This level of vulnerability is painful at times. I never think that sharing the things I share is a mistake, and no one has ever said anything mean to me about what I share, but sometimes I wonder how they *really* feel. Or how they talk about us later. I bet it's not always nice. I much prefer people thinking that I have it all together.

Honestly, it's not the actual sharing that makes me nervous anymore. It's that, every once in a while, when I share details of my story, my offering is met with silence—as if I have not just shared the deepest part of my soul. Other times when I share, people default to minimizing my experience as a way of making it more acceptable. That's pretty painful, too. I know that it's not intentional but simply the result of people not knowing how to respond. But this is the risk we take in sharing our stories in order to keep the lines of communication open about mental-health topics. If I want a world where people around me are not afraid to share their mental-health journeys, then I need to model it. This is something I will continue to do, even if it's painful at times. The pain is always worth it.

I was helped early on by anyone brave enough to talk about their own experiences with psychosis, depression, and hospitalization. At times, I was barely hanging on, and the honesty of others is what kept me able to move forward. I want to help other people move forward now, too. So, but for the cost of a bit of pride, I now get to be part of making sure that other people won't walk this path alone. Not in my circle, not on my watch.

Pieces

Brain broke
Hearts broke
He broke
She broke
God broke
Life broke

Into pieces
So tiny
And jagged
Never
To be glued
Back together
Again

And the scattered
Pieces sat
For years

And later
The pieces
Pressed together
Where they lay
To form
Something new

Something
That tells
The story
Of being broken

And sometimes
When the light shines
On the fragments
Just right
You can see
What was

See a striking
Resemblance
Of the old

In the shattered
Pieces
Of the
New

Heal

Sometimes
After black night
Light shines

Sometimes
After no air
Deep breaths

Sometimes
After bitter hurt
Calm

Sometimes
Endless pain
Ends

Sometimes
Unexpectedly
We heal

KEEPING IT REAL

I feel that true-to-life updates are important with stories like ours, so here is a difficult update that happened as I was writing this book. One might think that, after all these years, we would have it all figured out. Truthfully, for a while, life had reached a nice post-crisis equilibrium. We had painstakingly searched for and selected the most perfect therapist and psychiatrist, and all was working well. So well, in fact, that, after several consistent years of weekly appointments, Joe felt well enough to stop attending therapy. His therapist agreed—a lot of healing had transpired, and therapy is not intended to go on forever. We knew that this therapist was a phone call away should Joe ever need to return, so we all agreed it was time to stop attending sessions. Over the years, we stayed in touch with this therapist, updating him on our latest adventures. When we told our story publicly for the first time, Joe's therapist attended the presentation, and it was a gesture that neither of us will ever forget.

On the psychiatrist front, after a few med adjustments, Joe stabilized and did very well. Over seven years, the psychiatrist and Joe worked together to taper Joe down to one medication and keep him steady on the lowest dose. After many years of stability, Joe and his psychiatrist agreed that it would be a good time to see how Joe did without medication. They were ready to try this and fairly certain it would be successful. I was not. This back-and-forth discussion went on for a few years, and each time, I stood firm in my vote of "No." Given all that has happened, I was not—nor would I ever be—comfortable at the thought of living with unmedicated Joe. I thought it was unwise to take the chance, especially when things were going so well.

I was adamant in my assertion that I would not survive another Joe breakdown. Or—to be more blunt—*I* would absolutely survive another Joe breakdown, but *our marriage* would not. I let Joe know that I had precisely a one-shot reserve of energy for both surviving a trauma like the one I had gone through *and* for rebuilding a life from scratch. That reserve was now empty. It is a very serious proposition to consider tapering off of medication, not knowing if the symptoms will return. Was such an experiment worth risking our marriage? Over and over, my response was, *If you feel confident enough to gamble our marriage on the fact that you will be well without medication, give it a try, but I won't be sticking around again if you break.* More specifically (because I am a detail girl), I made it clear that, should the worst happen, I would be staying in the house, and *he* would need to find a place to live—so he should have a worst-case-scenario housing plan for himself solidly in place.

Ten full years after the initial episode, I had a change of heart. What can I say? They wore me down with logic. This wasn't going to be an unsupervised taper . . . this was going to be well planned and monitored by a psychiatrist we both respected. Joe's psychiatrist knew him very well by that point and had always been true to his word that I could call him at any time with any concerns. If Joe's behaviors changed even slightly, I felt confident that his psychiatrist would pick up on this quickly, and back on the med he would go. So we set up a safe, slow, and steady plan to taper Joe off medication.

This feels like progress, right? Joe doing great. A therapist who knows us well on call at any time. A psychiatrist who knows us well, with Joe's best interests in mind, walking us through tapering off meds. It seemed like the most solid of plans—but life, as we all know, has a mind of its own.

In Spring of that year, Joe's beautiful therapist, John, who had undergone a liver transplant the year prior, passed away from complications. It was a heartbreaking loss. We watched his memorial service online, as was standard practice during Covid times, and we mourned the loss of this incredible human who had walked with us through so much pain and helped Joe get to the healthy place he is in today. We will never think of him without being filled with gratitude.

During the Summer of that same year, we were blindsided with the devastating news that Joe's beloved psychiatrist Russell had passed away suddenly from heart complications. This news hit us like a brick. The loss of this remarkable man—who had put his heart and soul into knowing Joe, listened to him deeply, and helped him navigate his way out of the darkness—was a hurt beyond words. Joe had tapered fully off medication just six weeks prior, and we were all in *watch, wait, and see* mode, monitoring progress and watching Joe closely to make sure he stayed okay.

I was both shattered and scared. How could I not be? After the loss of his original therapist in the Spring, one of the conditions of tapering off medications was that Joe find a new therapist, one with whom he could meet with weekly to help process the change and to keep an eye out for returning symptoms of mania or depression. Luckily, by the time we learned of his psychiatrist's passing, Joe had already been meeting with a new therapist weekly for a few months. Also mercifully, a psychiatrist—from the same practice as the psychiatrist we had lost so tragically—agreed to keep seeing Joe as he adjusted to no medications. I was grateful and relieved that we were able to establish care with new providers so quickly, but I also deeply mourned that we no longer had a team in place with a long history of knowing Joe well. It was absolutely terrifying. The all-important-to-our-lives question, "Will Joe be okay without medication?" was one that could be answered only over time. I could only hope that a medication-free Joe would do well and that, if symptoms returned, we would catch them early.

As of this writing, it's been a successful medication-free three years so far, and all signs point to the shocking fact that Joe is now fine without medication. He has done a lot of work to rebuild the broken parts of his life, and he remains stable. Also, if his symptoms ever *do* return, we know which medicine works, and we'll have no shame in returning to it.

I know that John and Russell are smiling down on us so big right now. They never gave up on us, and we will never forget them. How fortunate we were that our paths crossed.

For John and Russell

You stood with us in the darkness, walked beside us toward the light, and helped us believe that life could be good again.

If you ever doubted that your lives here mattered, please know that they did.

We live well now: whole again, moving forward, hoping someday we can be to others what you have been to us.

You Don't Get to Know

You don't
Get to know
What's next

None of us do

Betrayal
Devastation
Disappointment

Peace
Contentment
Joy

Divorce
Death
Disability

Good Health
Rich friendships
Solid finances

We don't get to know
And we can't change
What's coming

Not through prayer
Or good wishes
Or right living

What comes
Comes

What goes
Goes

And the story
Of our lives

Is written
As life unfolds

And we get to read it
As the ink is drying

And not
One moment
Before

Section III

Beliefs

RELEASING BELIEFS

When mental-health issues entered our life, they impacted every part of it. Nothing was off limits. As mentioned earlier, part of Joe's original break involved religious delusions, which culminated in him thinking that he was God. We were fairly religious people before this happened, so it only makes sense that, when his brain got sick, it targeted and distorted thoughts around the topics that he thought about the most.

In order for me to heal, the way I thought about God had to change. This wasn't optional. If your brain has ever tricked you into believing you were God, or if you have ever been hurt—or even threatened—by someone claiming *they* were God, you, too, would have to change everything you believe about God. Trust me on this one. Joe's unraveling and all that went with it—the police, the terror, witnessing the disintegration of logical thought patterns in someone I loved—was brutal and damaging. Equally painful was the work of shedding long-held beliefs that no longer served me.

That no longer serve anyone whose life has imploded in this way.

At first, I tried my very best to use the beliefs I was raised with to guide me through this extremely complicated and painful new life. After a while, I realized that these beliefs were leading me in circles and deeper into pain. My old beliefs about assigning pain a higher purpose and keeping pain pretty were some of the most damaging.

Higher Purpose

The particular brand of faith I grew up with taught that everything that happens in life—no matter how awful—is for a higher purpose, for some greater good. I was taught that the most noble way to deal with pain was to "have faith through it" and to literally say things like "Though he slay me, yet will I trust Him" about what God was so clearly allowing. Whatever the issue, this was the approved response.

I didn't realize what was missing in this belief system until I found myself in such an exquisite level of pain. What was missing was permission to feel what I actually felt. There was absolutely no space allotted in my faith for yelling "WHATTTT THE FUCCCCK???" which is pretty much all you can yell for a long while at first.

There was no container large enough for that level of pain within my own faith at the time.

The answers available from my Christian toolbox were no longer adequate. They were weak whispers that could not compete with my hellish reality.

Side note: Readers from the brand of faith I came from are now, no doubt, concerned that I just used "... the F word." *Concerned that the use of this word symbolizes a falling away from God and all things good. I used to think the same. I used to be distracted by what I thought of as outer signs that someone didn't have a close relationship with God (e.g., swearing, not going to church, etc.). The thing is, we don't get to determine the inner workings of someone else's faith journey. My life no longer checks the boxes of my old faith, but God and I . . . we are fine.*

Pretty Pain

I had been rewarded for handling pain well in the past and had always been taught to make pain pretty.

I had witnessed people handling pain gracefully throughout my life, so I knew that it could be done. It was so inspiring to watch someone live with courage and positivity through something I couldn't picture myself surviving. It was something I aspired to.

I'd always been a pretty positive person, and, at the start of our crisis, though pain wrapped itself around me, I carried hopefulness in my back pocket. As time went on and things continued to get worse, the losses in my life built upon each other and gained momentum. My pockets emptied. Turned inside out. I couldn't contain hope or a positive outlook because I was actively just trying to survive.

I could no longer give those on the outside looking in what they wanted. When well-meaning others reminded me that my circumstance was part of God's plan, it felt like just another way for people to minimize my pain and distance themselves from it. When I let people get a glimpse of exhausted, angry, not-so-positive Becky, they stepped back, not knowing what to do with a front-row seat to ongoing devastation. I was too tired to make what I was living through look pretty.

The pain that rolled into our lives as a result of mental-health issues was a four-year tsunami. It almost drowned me, but I made it. I stayed above water. I thrashed and choked and grabbed hold of whatever I passed in the current; then I lost my grip and choked and thrashed again, grabbing hold of the next thing. This upset people who needed my pain to be easier to look at. I know it upset them, because, when they realized they were powerless to fix our situation, instead of coming closer and acknowledging the horror of it all with me, they doubled down on their *God's plan* assertions and continued to offer me tools from a toolbox that no longer worked for me. I was the one who was drowning, but I felt the weight of knowing that what I was going through was not easy to watch or to reconcile. And it seemed especially hard for my Christian friends, who desperately needed my messy situation to resolve so it could somehow be labeled and categorized as a testimony to God's grace. I wouldn't—couldn't—give that to people.

Instead, I questioned everything that those in faith communities around me found sacred. There was no more "sacred" to me. The *This pain is for your greater good* and *Pain handled well is noble* narratives no longer worked for my reality.

Where

God
Your word is
Mysteriously and Frustratingly
Lacking in
Detail

"In the course of my life He broke my
strength"
"He tears me down on every side till I am
gone; He uproots my hope like a tree"
"You have put me in the lowest pit, in the
darkest depths"

And then . . .

"The heavens are the work of your hands"
"I know that you can do all things"
Or no further mention of the person—
or the pain

Your word includes A and then Z
The beginning and then the end
Where is the middle?
Where is B through Y?

Where is the struggle to survive?
Where is the battle for peace?
Where is the trying to move forward through the pain?
Where is the thing that happens
To make people think You are good again?
To make people decide You are not useless or cruel?

Leaving that out is like
Giving someone a map
With the middle cut out
Or a book
With the important chapters
Missing

It's cheating

If I figure out
What it is
That gets people
From broken
To whole
I will include it

I won't hide
The dark, ugly
Middle part
Where the work is done

I won't hide
The detail between
"You failed me"
And "yet will I praise you"

I will include what is missing
So that the broken
Who come after me
Won't feel
So alone

In the course of my life he broke my strength
Psalm 102:23

He tears me down on every side till I am gone;
he uproots my hope like a tree
Job 19:10

You have put me in the lowest pit, in the darkest depths
Psalm 88:6

Could Have

You could have allowed just blindness
And we'd have found the resources to cope

You could have allowed just depression
And wise counsel would have eventually set things right

You could have allowed just trauma
And enough time to work it through

You could have allowed just delusion
That would have been more than enough

You could have allowed just a marriage broken
And we would have spent a lifetime piecing it back together

But in your infinite mercy
You gave us all of it

And then stood back and watched

As we fought for our lives

Thank you?

God as Companion

Once I'd let go of the pressure to assign a purpose to my pain or make it pretty, I had to revisit what I believed God's role in my pain was.

By necessity, I had to let go of the idea that God protects people from devastation. I had previously believed that God allowed pain into people's lives but that any allowed pain would be manageable, kept at a level that would give wisdom but not completely shatter. Even the pain of blindness—sad as it was—seemed like it was something that we could work with. That's why it was so easy to keep the pain pretty. Up until mental-health issues entered our lives, the pain I had personally experienced in life—though deep at times—was not overwhelming and was always redeemable in some way. Once my own life was shattered with wisdom-less unredeemable pain, I had to rethink this perspective.

At first, I had no idea how long the pain would last and was certain that relief must be right around the corner.

I was wrong.

Our lives not only didn't get better after that first crisis day—they got exponentially worse. He was in and out of hospitals. I never knew from one day to the next what kind of husband I'd come home to. Delusional, suicidal, something in between. Living with him was impossible, finding providers was impossible, and paying for care was impossible. This wasn't going to be a one-time hiccup that caused brief inconvenience and then was resolved. This was going to be our new life for the long haul. Time passed. Not days. Not months. But several hellish years. The pain was not alleviated. No one swooped in to rescue us. Nope, not even God.

With the exception of the few times I looked up and shook my fists at the sky, I was too busy surviving to figure out what I really thought about God. My early poems—asking where God was and why God had "given" us so many impossible circumstances at one time—were the extent of my wrestling. I was deeply disappointed with God, but my hands were too full with day-to-day survival to process or respond. Tucked in the back of my mind, I had the thought, *I'll be back for you later, God, to revisit what's happened, but, right now, unless you can help alleviate this situation, I don't have time for this discussion.*

During that time, I read many books about others who were walking through ongoing fire. It was a relief to realize that not everyone believed that God was the gatekeeper for whether bad things were allowed into a life. Not everyone believed that pain was always used for a greater good. Not everyone believed that God was happier when you *handled pain in a noble fashion.*

I began to let myself think of God as a companion rather than protector. It was the only way I could keep God.

If you are still convinced that God does swoop in and stop devastation on a regular basis, maybe that's been true in your life, but it wasn't true in mine, and it's not true for many. I hope when this life is over, we will get to understand more about how it all works, but not now. In this life, my belief is that we have God's company if we want it. And God can be great company if there is no expectation of rescue.

Protecting

God of the details
Who knows each hair
On my head

Who answers
Specific and urgent requests

Who meets secret needs

That's
Not always true,
Is it?

Lots of times
Urgent prayers
Go unanswered

Lots of times
No needs are met
Be they secret or glaring

Lots of times
Specific or vague requests
Are not acknowledged

And that reality
Is okay

What's not okay
Is the insistence
On ignoring
The reality
Of a sometimes
Silent
God

On protecting God's reputation
As if that is needed

What's not okay
Is when we look reality
In the face
And deny it

When we do that
We are not protecting God

We are protecting
What we want
To be true
About God

Writing God's story

Instead of learning
From the story
God is telling

Explaining Away Pain

My life now does not allow me to minimize pain, to label it as worth it for some future glory, or to assign God as pain's source but not reconcile the implications.

It's okay if others don't agree with my decisions to let some of my old beliefs go. It's up to each of us to dig deep and determine what we truly believe. It's okay if beliefs differ.

It's not okay to disregard our doubts or leave unexamined our deep and valid concerns, and call accepting that which is unacceptable to us at the core "faith."

I ask a lot of questions now in relation to beliefs. For example, I wonder if those who say that "all things that happen are part of God's plan to be used for His glory" have ever actually traced this logic to its natural end. I wonder if anyone has asked parents who have lost children tragically if—even years later—they think it was for the best? And yes, I do believe something good has the potential to come from every tragedy, but that's different from claiming that the reason something horrific has happened is that, eventually, something positive might come from it. Wonderful foundations have been started in honor of lives lost too young to various diseases, but I would never insist that the loss of life was worth it so that a greater good could come of it. When something good comes from something awful, it's typically the result of a lot of hard work and healing on the part of those left behind. We don't get to use the good that came from something bad as validation for why it happened, especially when we are not the ones it happened to.

I very quickly found that whenever I pushed back against a belief that no longer made sense to me, the pushback wasn't welcomed. If I questioned the logic that "God never gives us more than we can handle" by referencing the many who die by suicide, I was met with blank stares. If someone claimed that even the most horrible circumstances can be used for God's glory, I would ask specifically what the glory outcome was in the Sandy Hook murders, because I seem to have missed it. I was amazed at how easily other people's pain could be explained away by people who didn't have to feel a bit of it.

As much as I was frustrated by the overly simplified answers being thrown at my own incredibly complicated circumstance, I was also angry at myself for never before this time questioning the logic of my beliefs. I raged at how easily my fellow Christians attempted to "faithsplain" away my pain, knowing that I had likely offered the same trite explanations to others in the past.

SIDELINES

Surviving our life and simultaneously trying to forge new beliefs—while those with old beliefs watched—felt like a Mack truck with four sets of wheels coming at us, with no chance of escape.

As the first set of wheels ran over us, from the sidewalk—the sidelines, really—we could hear, "We are praying for you," "God is with you" comments yelled in our direction. These comments are trademark of Christians everywhere early in crisis situations.

And as we lay there half crushed, watching the second set of wheels approaching, again the comments from the sidelines came, but this time it was, "This is for your good," "God has a plan." Again, the wheels crushed us.

By the time the third set of wheels came, with what little strength we had left, we started to yell back, "Please stop with your comments. They fall short. You there on the sidewalk have no idea of what it's like to be us here on the pavement."

By the time the fourth set of wheels hit us, the sidewalk watchers were gone, scattered away, after realizing they could not reconcile the only words of comfort they knew how to provide with the reality that was happening right in front of them.

And then it was mercifully quiet.

And we survived.

We did the difficult work of rebuilding our bodies, minds, and souls. We came to new conclusions about how this life works, how faith works, and how God works based on our own personal lived experience.

We finally again felt peace.

And then the people who had run off when the fourth set of wheels hit . . . the ones who couldn't reconcile reality with book knowledge . . . the ones who went away . . . started yelling again from the sidelines. They said things like: "What you believe is not right," "We have never been asked to endure—much less survive—what you did, but we know it works only in the way we say it works."

And we kept walking. And we didn't look back.

You don't get to weigh in on what you have not experienced.

You don't get to come to conclusions on matters you have not cared to witness up close.

You yellers on the sidewalk still think that you have all the answers. And we can only look at you with a sort of sad awe for all that life still has to teach you.

LEAVING CHURCH

We were different versions of us before mental-health issues arrived.

We had been active members of our church.

Our social lives outside of work had involved attending church and hanging out primarily with others who also went to church. It was a pretty closed circle, but it didn't feel like it at the time.

We were on a worship team, which means we loved singing and playing contemporary Christian music, and helped lead singing at church whenever needed.

I grew up in church, the daughter of a pastor. This meant I went to church twice on Sundays, every Wednesday, and then to youth group on Friday. My social life was church.

My extended family and friends went to church.

Church was a safe place from this scary world, and my upbringing ensured that I was planted firmly within it.

Joe came to church later in life, after a bit of a turbulent childhood and some issues with addiction. Finding God freed him from a lot of his past issues. He was pretty much a prodigal-son success story.

We met at a church youth group. We were happy, positive people and made a perfect pair.

I learned a lot in church and had a deep and personal faith.

I cannot overemphasize the role that church and evangelical Christianity played in my life and in forming my world view.

I haven't been to church in years.

I really tried to make it work. Tried to reconcile what I'd been taught about how God works with the new life that had been dropped on me.

Maintaining a white-knuckle death grip on beliefs that didn't fit my reality anymore was admirable for a while—and then it was just plain stupid. When I finally let old beliefs go, my pain was instantly relieved. But this decision caused the pain of those in my old faith community to increase. They felt scared for me, angry at me for questioning, and threatened by me. They wanted me to hold tightly to beliefs that were no longer true for me, and I could not do that. The biggest thing we had in common—our shared beliefs—was removed, and, as a result, the glue of our relationship disappeared. Many of these friendships faded into the background. For friends who stuck around, there was strain on both sides when we met up: them wondering about our souls and us hoping for some grace. As much as we wanted them to understand why our beliefs had to change, we didn't want them to have to endure what it would take to do so.

Up until that point, I had always been able to reconcile what I'd been taught in church with the life I was living. But when my world imploded, I could no longer make the pieces fit. I couldn't sit in church every week and listen to teachings that could not be applied to my life. The words might as well have been spoken in a foreign language. There was nowhere for them to land.

Unravel

I want
To be free
To unravel

All my
Tightly held
Beliefs

As needed

Again and again

My whole life through

I want
The freedom
Every so often
To release my grip
On what I think is true

To let that truth
Stand on its own
Without me

To stand back and rethink it
See if I still believe it

Then pick it up again
And live it

Or set it free
And make room
For something deeper

LOSING ACCEPTANCE

A Good Follower

I was born with a soft-spoken nature. Growing up, I thoroughly enjoyed learning and following the rules set before me (school, church, speed limits—you name it, I followed it). In a world that could be scary to navigate, I was grateful for instructions. I thought that if I followed them, they would lead me to the life I was meant to have. I was such a good follower.

In school, I enjoyed the recognition that being a good student brought me.

In my social life, my unassuming personality helped me fit in just about anywhere.

At church, I fit in beautifully. I loved learning and, by nature, loved to listen and give.

I wrote poems and songs about how I believed faith and God worked and about how I believed the world worked. I surrounded myself with people who believed the exact same thing. If people in my life went through hard times, I interpreted their situations through the narrow lens of reasoning that I had been taught, which included the dual narratives that everything that happens is part of God's master plan and that pain is an opportunity to bring glory to God. I didn't yet know that not every trauma could be managed by "giving it to God and covering it with prayer." I didn't know some traumas were just too big. Looking back now, I can't think of anyone in my faith community who lived through a deep trauma, stayed in church, and also openly expressed rage or demanded more from their faith. To have the support of the faith community, any expression of pain had to fall within acceptable boundaries. If you don't think that's true, think about how many people in your faith community openly and ongoingly express rage at the pain that enters their lives.

My parents could not have been prouder of me throughout my growing-up years as I checked off all the *good-daughter* boxes: good Christian, good student, good person. For most of my life, this is who I authentically was.

Then my life changed. My world disintegrated from within. I lost myself. Lost my husband. Lost God. Lost my faith community. Along with this, I lost acceptance. I never knew how deeply I was enmeshed in my particular brand of faith until I walked toward the boundaries of it and pushed through. I had always felt that I was accepted as I was. Always felt surrounded by support. As I changed my beliefs and distanced myself from church, I watched as acceptance turned to disappointment and even anger.

The Realm of the Disapproved

It is exceptionally painful to look into the eyes of people who once admired everything about you and know that they don't approve of who you have become or how your beliefs have changed. It's painful to look into someone's eyes and see how badly they want you to be someone or something else.

It was hard for me—someone who lived to please and who had a large part of her self-esteem generated externally. People in my life were a mirror for my worth, and, when they became disappointed with me, I felt like I had failed them. There was no going back to my old beliefs, though. No going back to church. This was not an option. I was moving forward the only way I knew how, and, instead of feeling supported in my journey, as I always had been, I felt judged. When I answered the question "Where are you going to church now" with the truth, which was "Nowhere," any progress I would go on to describe in my life from that point forward was discounted. The only thing that mattered was that I wasn't checking off the box that said "good Christian."

There was no curiosity as to why I wasn't going to church. No regard for how a mental break, complete with the trauma of religious psychosis, could play any part in needing distance from church. No invite for deeper discussion on the many parts of my faith I'd painstakingly had to rethink to get to the healthy place I was in at that moment. It was a painful experience to realize that the main reason I was accepted before was that I was compliant. I was accepted for the way I believed and for the way I didn't make waves. Accepted for my silence and my ability to accept what I was taught without needing to question.

Giving up old beliefs has consequences. My changed beliefs made those around me who didn't have need of a wider faith very uncomfortable. It's not like deciding you like a different flavor of ice cream. It's deciding differently about the way you think the universe is structured and, by doing that, rejecting how others might think it is structured. It became an effort to be around those who believed the way I used to because, quite honestly . . . they wanted me to believe the way I used to. They had no practice in making space for a new way of believing. They no longer wanted to know me. They wanted only to encapsulate the old version of me. A version that no longer existed. When it became clear that people from my past weren't interested in my widened beliefs—much less the life experiences that brought me to them—I tried not to talk about my new life around them. But deciding not to talk about what makes you *you* is not a long-term solution.

I had never before experienced the torment of not being invited to bring my whole self to the table. Or of being actively invited to suppress the most important parts of my life, ensuring that they never made it to the table at all—the table of life or the literal dinner table. Dear God, whatever you do, don't bring this shit up at dinner.

Growing up, I never gave much thought to the groups of people that the religion of my youth considered outsiders. Why would I, when I was safely, warmly, and oh-so-very-cozily resting inside the inner circle of acceptance? It wasn't until I questioned my beliefs and left some behind that I felt the sting—the full-on rejection. I no longer attended church. I no longer believed that God was in control of what happens to us. I no longer believed that I had to say my pain was worth it to make God happy. I felt exactly zero guilt about any of it. Any time I attempted to share even the tiniest parts of my updated beliefs, I could immediately feel the walls go up.

As a kid, I was always taught to be careful around people who didn't believe the same as we did, to not get caught up in the ways of the world. Now I *was* the world. I had to be kept on the outside. I mean, it's not like I wanted to get back on the inside, anyway. I just wanted to respectfully co-exist. But how can you co-exist with people who think you are a bad person? Or worse yet, how can you co-exist with people who can't acknowledge that what you've been through has changed everything? Who can't see the beauty in the life you've built back from the ashes? To those I had shared the same faith with for decades, I had done the unthinkable. I had practiced my faith for years—and then reexamined it in light of the events of my life and decided to leave large parts of it behind. That's actually much worse than someone who is on the outside because they've never believed at all. My rejection of the beliefs I'd grown up with was much more insulting. So those who had once held me in high regard for believing so well no longer did. No longer one of them, I was relegated to the realm of the disapproved.

What's Unspoken

When people feel that someone else is dangerously, life-threateningly wrong—living wrong, believing wrong, making wrong decisions about everything from faith to politics—that concern becomes all consuming. The intensity lurks in the background of even the most mundane conversations (Me: "What should we order for dinner?" Intensely Concerned Person: "Pasta and also, *Do you know you're on the red-hot road to Hell?*"). Conversations feel stilted, like there is always something important left unsaid. Don't get me wrong, I make zero apologies for the gorgeous life I lead now, and I certainly don't want to feel like the subject of an intervention during every conversation simply because I have a wider faith. But there is a strange "fear energy" around people who don't or can't say what they mean. The energy is shallow, empty, and unable to engage in thought-provoking conversation. There is no depth of relationship around inauthentic energy. Nothing is watered. Nothing grows deeper.

I found that I was about as welcome to be fully me around people from my old faith as I would imagine gay and lesbian people are to be fully themselves in churches that simultaneously condemn homosexuality and assure newcomers that all are welcome. Welcome to come if they stay silent. Welcome to come but not bring their whole selves.

It's uncomfortable when all that is unspoken is put into actual words, but maybe we should do this more often, so that there is no confusion about the messages being communicated. Honesty might sound more like:

- "You can come here, but we believe you are wrong and going to hell."
- "You can believe differently from me, but I am right, and you are wrong."
- "I can no longer be close friends with you because I'm afraid that your different beliefs will lead me away from God—and I can't take that chance."
- "Because you have decided to believe differently from me, part of our friendship now means that you must allow me to continually try to convince you to see things my way, because a tenet of my faith is to bring those around me into my exact faith."

As much as I love the idea of making the unspoken spoken, learning the truth about how someone feels about you can be pretty painful. I learned this the hard way when I shared with someone that I had changed my mind about an old belief. It took this person by surprise, and, with no cleaned-up response at the ready, the truth of how they felt came out. I found myself on the receiving end of a clumsy yet incredibly painful diatribe about how far off-track they felt I had fallen, how poor my judgment was, and how much easier the old me was for them to accept. In that short interaction, the strange "silence energy" that had become standard in that relationship all of a sudden found words, and the words were callous. Those scorching words tried to incinerate the many years of work I had done while walking through hell to come out on the other side with a faith that was my own. Tried to push me back into silent compliance. Tried to negate my hard-fought journey. Tried but did not succeed.

That conversation was both painful and telling.

When you think that you are right and that no one else can be right unless they see things like you do, there is no room for conversation. No way of knowing a person well. No space for curiosity or vulnerability. No depth of connection. It makes sense, then, why efforts to grow relationships in this environment aren't successful.

If we were better at putting words to what's unspoken, we could probably all save ourselves a lot of time and heartbreak, as it would be clear which relationships were sustainable and which might need to be given space.

Exclusion

Many (but thankfully not all) faith communities are unwavering in their exclusion. They believe very specifically that:

- Their translation of the Bible is the only right one
- Faith put into action looks a very specific way
- Sundays are intended for communing with like believers
- The significant investment of time required to keep the church machine in motion is a non-negotiable
- There is an Us and a Them, a Saved and a Condemned—that the warm glow of family can be among only the Us, who share these common beliefs

This becomes a problem when you leave the faith because:

- Faith enacted outside of the structure of the church and church community is invalidated
- Relationships between people of different beliefs could not possibly be sustainable when one is sure they're right

It's all downright exhausting to navigate.

A lot of us have friends or family who believe differently on a whole spectrum of topics, and we work it out.

But religion seems to be a deal-breaker.

So we do our best.

We make the effort.

We try to keep ourselves whole in the process.

ACCEPTANCE

I learned pretty quickly that people didn't like when I refused to accept simple explanations for my complicated life. People didn't like the Becky who spoke about her ongoing pain. People didn't like when I called them out on their desire to rewrite my story in a way that wasn't true for me. People didn't like me as much. They accepted the version of me they wanted me to be, but they did not accept me in my truest form.

So I went ahead and accepted me for them.

I realize that it is hard to see people change and grow. And because I shared roots with those who were closely connected with me, my roots being pulled up tugged on their roots, too, at times leaving messy open space in their spiritual landscapes. The changes I needed to make had the ripple effect of suggesting that those around me might want to reexamine their own beliefs, too. I had upset the *status quo*, and people don't like their *quo* messed with.

Some decided I was angry at God.

Others decided I was being led astray.

Some were angry at me for not using this devastating experience as a testimony.

Some wanted me to demonstrate more faith.

None of these people were living my story. Most didn't care to get their hands dirty with the painful day-to-day details of what we were dealing with. Many came at me with a pre-packaged answer—who cares what the question was—and were offended when I returned the answer unwrapped. Oddly, those who seemed to judge me most harshly were the same people who couldn't bear to look me or my pain in the eyes.

As much as I disappointed people, they also disappointed me. I had never realized the lengths to which we will go to hold onto a story we don't want to change.

Outside the Inner Circle

Inside
The well-contained
Solid boundaries
Of the inner circle
There were so many questions
I had no answers for
But thought someone
Wiser,
Further along on the journey,
Did,
Must

Outside
The inner circle
Which had grown too small
Still many questions
I have no answers for
But I know now that
No one really does
No matter how long
They've been on the journey
No matter what
They tell you

And I am every day more okay with this
Because not knowing it all for sure
And saying so
And living with that
Is a huge relief

And the questions are brilliant
And the asking is brave

And though the inner circle
Is filled with good, smart people

Good, smart people are
Here with me now, too
Lots of them

Standing room only
Outside the inner circle

When people from my old faith saw my beliefs changing, there wasn't much talk about it. I think that was one of the most surprising things for me. No one asked me for details about how my life was changing or about the process by which I was coming to new conclusions about God. They just knew that I no longer checked all the boxes (church attendance was a big one)—and that was all they needed to know. If I could have just found it within myself to return to church—even if I didn't believe what I heard there—that simple act would have put everyone at ease. And that level of misguidedness is why I had to break free.

Come Around

No discussion
No intent
To understand

Just Do you
Believe yet
Exactly as
I do?

And if not
I don't need
To know more

But I will
Check in
Again later

To see
If you've
Come around

Brokenness is uncomfortable to experience and uncomfortable to watch. When it goes on too long, sometimes people on the outside looking in have to either walk away or create a narrative around why it might be happening. Very few are able to just sit alongside and acknowledge an ongoing pain. I lived broken for years, but I didn't feel like I was allowed to admit that in certain faith circles. My old beliefs about the most noble way to handle pain also made honoring the ongoing pain in myself really hard. I'm glad I can just name my pain now and experience it without shame.

Allowed to Be Broken

Interesting distinction
How we are allowed to be *broken*
From divorce, death, loss of all kinds
But not allowed to stay *broken*

Or have brokenness alter beliefs
Or have it forever change us

We are allowed to be broken
As long we recover well and quickly
And let everyone know God had a plan
So the suffering was bearable

Allowed to be broken
If the brokenness
Is contained
And not too disturbing to witness

But that's not really
Being allowed
To be broken

Acceptance

Being allowed to be broken
Means honoring that
My brokenness has changed me
And that my brokenness
Might change you

Being allowed to be broken
Means recognizing that
I have a difficult road to walk
Whether you come with me or not
And I might not be back

Being allowed to be broken
Means listening when I say
This is what I see here
Whether you see it or not

It just strikes me
That I always thought
Brokenness was allowed
Until I broke and learned
Otherwise

KEYNOTE

It was painful to be on the receiving end of well-meaning but functionally useless advice. I don't think God would give advice like the kind of advice that came my way. I think God would fire at least half his spokespeople if given the chance.

I recently joined a group of people who have in common caring for a disabled spouse. There are almost a thousand members in the online group alone and who knows how many more offline. Hundreds upon hundreds all doing the day-to-day—often thankless—work of keeping ill spouses fed, clothed, entertained, hopeful, and alive. Most of these people are young (between ages 30 and 60). Some are new to caregiving, while others have been at it for 15 to 20 years or more. Some of the illnesses are physical, others are mental, and some are a lovely combination of both. For most, the spouse's disability was an unexpected event. *Life happened* and required them to give care, so they do.

This group holds a huge conference every year. People come from all around. Speakers are brought in, and, for a few days, caregivers are surrounded by others who understand what it's like to wonder how you will survive another day, to dream about a day when this will be over, to sacrifice everything you are to keep the family afloat only to be criticized by an ungrateful spouse who needs someone to yell at and finds you an easy target.

I wondered the other day, *If God was asked to come and give the keynote address to this group, what would it be like?* Would God stand before a group of thousands of battle-scarred caregivers and say with a smile "This is for my glory"? Would God say to those married to once-healthy men whose diapers they are now changing, "I can heal this but opt not to because I am refining you"? Would God say to the husband who has spent the last 15 years being berated daily by his dementia-diagnosed wife, "Just give it time, and you will see it all works for my good"? Would God say to the woman who has missed countless important life events, including the birth of her grandchild, because she cannot find anyone who will enter her life for even a day to give her respite . . . would God really say "Keep it positive and people will be drawn to me through this"?

I don't think so.

I don't think God would say any of these things. So why do we say these things to each other?

When people of faith get a glimpse into my life, if they stick around at all, the most common reaction they have is to offer surface assurances that don't tie back to my reality. They sound like this: *Hold tight—God will use this; Give it time, and you'll see this is all for God's glory; God is refining you; We must trust what God allows; God doesn't give us more than we can handle.* I can think of nothing more lonely when your world has fallen down than to hear words like this from those who are on top of their own worlds. Words like this can only be said from a distance. They are well-intentioned—yet misinformed—words. My guess is that it would take just a few days—of enduring insult from a sick spouse, changing adult diapers, or forfeiting the joys in life to care for one who doesn't want to live—for these words to dry up, for the speakers of these words to stand in silent awe of the firsthand reality of suffering.

And that silence might just be the beginning of something useful, might just be the most comforting sound the sufferer has heard in a long time.

What would God say as a keynote speaker? I think God would stand before these spouses with tears and say, "I love you so much. I see your brokenness. I am in awe of your courage. My heart is torn for you and for this situation and for the broken world in which you live. And someday, this broken world will be put back together—but probably not in your lifetime. Probably the life before you now is the life you will have. And I do not ask you to celebrate it, only to live it the best you can. I have found you here on Earth doing the holy work of my hands. And I ask you through the blinding pain of your days to find God any way you can. It doesn't have to be in a church with those who don't know this life. It doesn't even have to be in the ways you've known before. But please don't give up the search. Find God in the beauty of the November morning skies. Find God as you lean on each other. Find God in early-morning silence before anyone needs you. Find God in the unexpected kindness of those who don't wear a religious label. Live these days as best you can, dear ones, and find me any way you can."

A NEW LIFE SCRIPT

When mental-health issues arrived, the life we had known before that time officially ended. It was like driving over a bridge on a sunny day, hearing an explosion, and looking back to see that the bridge had collapsed in full. It wasn't a matter of not wanting to return to our old beliefs and ways—at first, we really did try. It was that going backwards wasn't an option and there was no other way to go but forward.

Like trying to complete a puzzle when the box is missing pieces, the effort I spent trying to make the details of my story fit my faith were futile.

I had to get up from the table and leave the puzzle unfinished.

In the process, I dismantled my old restrictive beliefs about the purpose of pain or the nobility of making pain pretty. I stopped thinking of God as a bodyguard and started thinking of God as companion. I left church.

So what does a person who has just released her grip on all of her old beliefs do next?

I'm glad you asked.

She changes her approach.

Instead of making my story fit into the faith I was raised with, I asked my faith to expand to fit the story I was living.

Peace started returning to my life when I let go of *everything that I'd been taught* about how God works and started *watching my actual life* to learn how God works. What I see now, based on my experience, is that, though God may walk beside me through the horrors of my life, God does not stop them. And there is no mandate to walk through pain gracefully. You get through it however you can. I also came to understand that it doesn't matter who is praying and how fervently. God doesn't pick and choose whose suffering is worthy enough to end that way. What a monstrous God that would be—one who doesn't help because someone didn't pray hard enough.

I found freedom in allowing my beliefs to be shaped by what was true in my own life, rather than what might be true in other people's lives.

This change felt like a big exhale after way too much time holding my breath.

This change marked the first time I had ever trusted myself enough to ask more from my faith.

It was terrifying.

It was lonely.

It was absolutely the right path for me.

I'm living a brand-new life script now.

So what does life look like these days? I pretty much just spend my days sinning. That was a joke. What life looks like now *is life*. I'm happy. I'm at peace. I feel good about what I believe now and allow for the reality that what I believe might change again over time as my life unfolds. I don't have it all figured out. I never will. No one ever will, actually, despite what they tell you.

Nothing I say will ever be enough for those who want my life to look like it did before. If I say I find God everywhere, I will be reminded that I should find God in church. If I say God and I are good, I will be asked about specific beliefs that are truly no one else's business. People may judge me, but I don't feel the need to explain myself anymore. I'm not trying to keep any faith-club-membership card in good standing. I'm not trying to impress anyone. I'm too busy living.

In those carefree months before mental-health issues arrived, I was oblivious to the devastation that was about to come into my life and to the devastation that other lives had experienced well before me. I feel like God knew what was coming, though. I feel like God was as devasted as I was at the events that played out.

Did You Know?

Did you know
Way back then,
God,
The years
That were ahead
For me?

Could you see
What was coming?

Did your heart break, too,
Days prior,
When you witnessed
My carefree spirit

Knowing

It was the last
You'd see that
For a while?

I sometimes wonder
If I *would have wanted*
To see
It coming

A New Life Script

If I would have benefited
From some strong inner
voice

Warning me
That something life-changing
Was on my doorstep

Telling me
To brace myself

To get one last
Good laugh in
While I could

There is wisdom in people's pain. If we are lucky, people in pain will share it with us.

True

I cringe sometimes
When people tell me
What is true

In a way
That's true only
For them

Because,
If what
You believe
About God
Isn't true
For everyone,
Every day
Of the year

Then
It is not
True

If what is true
The day
Your house
Was built
Isn't true
The day your house
Burns down

A New Life Script

It isn't
True

If what is true
The day
Your baby
Is born
Isn't true
The day your baby
Is lost

It isn't
True

Still, it's hard
For people
Who are sure

That their true
Is truer
Than mine

To admit that
Lives are different

Making thoughts
On truth
Different, too

Prayer is different for me now. No more prayer with the belief that God might swoop in and intervene. Just prayer as a reminder that God works through people to make life tolerable, and, if anything, prayer is just a reminder to listen for how you might help.

If I Prayed

If I prayed
I wouldn't pray
For God to fix
A situation

But I would pray
For God
To fix
Me

If I prayed
I wouldn't pray
For God to stop
Life's ebb and flow

But I would pray
God help me handle
What goes on here

I'd pray
Don't fix the world—
Fix me

I'd pray
Don't change the world—
Change me

A New Life Script

Make me strong
In this world

And I will go out
And change it
Myself

My rebuilt faith is nothing like it was before. It's so much wider and more merciful. I can bring my whole self to it.

Respectful

I want to be respectful
Of the beliefs
Of my youth
And of those
Who still
Have them

I want to be respectful
Though my beliefs
Have changed
Expanded
To hold my life

I want to be respectful
Of all those
Around me

And at the same time—

This is
Important—

I want to
Be respectful
Of me

There is nothing like having complete peace with what I believe. No more will I carry the weight of other people's judgments about my personal beliefs. No more. I believe what I believe and only that. I am not threatened by the way anyone else chooses to believe. I trust that we all know ourselves well and believe in ways that make most sense to the lives we are living. I may not fit anymore into organized religion, but I fit into my own skin.

To Anyone Who Wonders

To anyone who wonders
What it feels like

To live out beliefs
That differ
From the masses'
But perfectly match
Your own

To take
A deep look
At long-held
Assumptions
And decide
To change
Your mind

It feels mostly brave

And sometimes lonely

And also ironic

To be close to God
And judged as not

But mostly
I have to say
It just feels good
To be free

Section IV

How It Ends

THE LIFE I'VE BEEN GIVEN

This was not what I had planned for my life. I did not plan for my blind husband to experience mental-health issues. I did not plan to walk away from the faith of my childhood. I did not plan to find God outside of church.

But does it really matter what any of us have planned?

I did not plan for the life I have, but this is the life I've been given.

And right now, it's not so bad.

My husband is well now. Still blind but mentally well. My beliefs fit my actual life. There is no duplicity. I bring my whole self to my whole life. I know myself well. Whatever heartaches life brings next, I'll be okay, because I have a belief system that makes sense now. I'll be okay, because I know what I've already survived. I know that I will make it through any future pain the same way I have made it through the hardest parts of my life thus far: When pain levels me, I will eventually get up.

I will acknowledge the pain and keep walking, one foot in front of the other, until I reach the peace I know is there, just waiting for me to arrive.

CLOSING THOUGHTS

Although it is impossible to describe the entirety of my or anyone else's experience in a handful of pages,

Impossible to include all the intricacies of a life in such condensed space,

I hope these words have left you with a deeper understanding of the people in your life who may be navigating the murky waters of physical and/or mental challenges. I hope these words have left you with tender compassion for anyone whose life has demanded the re-evaluation of beliefs.

If that person is you,

I hope you see how strong you are.

I hope you know that your story matters.

POEMS

Beliefs

ABOUT THE AUTHOR

Becky LeBlanc lives her sometimes complicated yet generally beautiful life in Massachusetts. When she is not working her day job, she is a poet, writer, and conference speaker. She loves words, sunrises, and brutal honesty, because no one's life is as shiny as it looks online. This is her debut memoir.

You can reach her at: sometimesthingsfallapart@gmail.com.

www.ingramcontent.com/pod-product-compliance
Lightning Source LLC
LaVergne TN
LVHW022200200926
848481LV00006B/1790
* 9 7 8 0 9 7 5 9 2 5 8 2 9 *